the new cook

acknowledgments

With thanks to Matt Handbury and Jackie Frank, for such a brilliant opportunity; to Jane Roarty, for her inspiration and most passionate support; to Sara Beaney, a brilliant designer, for making my book beautiful; to Michèle, for all the weekends and late nights of toil; to Rowena, my editor, who kept me motivated; to Catie, Anne, Anna, Mark and all of the rest of the Murdoch Books team, for your patience and for such a great opportunity; to Mum and Dad, for the endless stream of support and understanding – I guess I'll always be a running-late sort of person – thanks for waiting; to my friends William and Sibella, who tasted and tested, and supported me through the book; to my partner and friend Billy – words can't describe – thanks; to Jody, my inspiration, colleague, friend, and strength, who enabled me to get this far – thank you; to the Antico family, for searching the markets for the most amazing fresh fruit and vegetables, and for entertaining me when I come to the shop; to Con and James of Demcos Seafood Providores, for the freshest, sweetest seafood; to Petrina, who stuck with the cracking pace, for the long and sometimes painful task of photography, thank you for your input and energy in making this book a visual feast.

Published by Murdoch Books®
Art Director/Designer: Sara Beaney
Recipes and Styling: Donna Hay
Photographer: Petrina Tinslay
Designer: Michèle Lichtenberger
Editor: Rowena Lennox
Additional Photography: William Meppem, p.37, p.84 right, p.107 top right, p.136; Quentin Bacon p.125, p.182.
White bowls, plates and accessories: Pillivuyt from Hale Imports, telephone (02) 9938 2400

Chief Executive: Juliet Rogers
Publisher: Kay Scarlett

A catalogue record for this book is available from the National Library of Australia
ISBN 0 86411 763 9.

Text © Donna Hay 1997. Design and photography © Murdoch Books® 1997.
Printed by Toppan Printing Hong Kong Co Ltd. First printed 1997. Reprinted 1998 (four times), 1999 (three times), 2000, 2002.
PRINTED IN CHINA

Published by:

AUSTRALIA
Murdoch Books® Australia
GPO Box 1203
Sydney NSW 1045
Phone: (612) 4352 7000
Fax: (612) 4352 7026

UK
Murdoch Books® UK
Ferry House
51– 57 Lacy Road
London SW15 1PR
Phone: (020) 8355 1480
Fax: (020) 8355 1499

the new cook

donna hay

MURDOCH
BOOKS

contents

introduction

Good food is a combination of fresh ingredients and uncomplicated layers of flavour. When you start with quality produce, a few simple flavours will complement and contrast with your base ingredients to create the perfect taste experience. Think of food with passion, not anxiety, and feel free to substitute and add ingredients as you please. This is often how personalised culinary masterpieces are created. More information about ingredients marked with a star* can be found in the glossary.

the new cook is your guide to quick preparation, easy cooking techniques and inventive serving ideas. Step-by-step recipes take you through the basics and lead you to a feast of easy-to-follow recipes with a signature.

eggs

basics

Eggs can be the most simple and the most difficult of foods to cook. When you understand a few basic properties of the humble egg, the mystery of cooking the perfect egg unravels.

selection and storage

I prefer true free-range eggs for their flavour, and for their bright yolks and thick whites. There are a few good reasons for storing eggs in their carton in the refrigerator. Egg shells are porous and they will absorb any strong food smells in your fridge. Eggs are packed with the pointed end down so the yolk stays centred and the air sac at the blunt end has less pressure on it and is not damaged. Storage life depends on the freshness of the eggs when purchased. Around 2 1/2–3 weeks is an egg's maximum fridge life.

boiling

For eggs at room temperature slipped into boiling water:
SOFT
2–3 minutes
FIRM WHITE,
SOFT YOLK
5–6 minutes
HARD BOILED
10 minutes
To centre the yolk, add the egg to water that has been stirred to create a whirlpool and continue stirring for 1 minute while cooking.

freshness

Freshness can be tested in two ways:
1 When it's cracked onto a plate, the yolk of a fresh egg will sit high and look plump and rounded. The fresh white should be thick and a little cloudy, and cling to the yolk.
2 Drop an egg into a bowl of water. If the egg floats on its side, it is fresh; if it floats vertically with the rounded end up, it is 2–3 weeks old. An egg that floats on the surface of the water has seen better days and should be filed in the rubbish bin. The larger the air pocket in the egg, the older it is.

poaching

I'm a self-confessed bad egg-poacher but I'm still trying! Have a 7–10cm (3–4 inch) frypan full of rapidly simmering water. Break each egg into a cup and gently slip the egg into the pan. Stir the rapidly simmering water to form a whirlpool for a neat oval-shaped poached egg. Allow the egg to cook for 3–4 minutes before removing it from the pan with a slotted spoon. To test for readiness, press the egg with your finger. The white should be firm and the yolk should be soft.

tips for success

It is sometimes better to use eggs at room temperature, especially when beating whole eggs or egg whites, or using them as an emulsifier. Eggs are extremely sensitive to heat and there may be only a minute between a tender, moist egg and a tough, dry, rubbery egg. When adding eggs to anything hot (such as soups), add a little of the hot substance to the eggs first. Salt relaxes the protein in eggs, making them easier to blend. However, if salt is added to eggs that are to be scrambled, poached or made into an omelette, the eggs will become thin and may break up when cooked.

scrambling

Start by melting a tablespoon of butter in a frypan over medium heat. Place 2 eggs in a bowl and whisk with 1–2 tablespoons of milk or cream. Pour eggs and milk into frypan and slowly stir with a wooden spoon. Stir just enough to break up the eggs but don't over stir so the eggs become a lumpy mass. Scrambled eggs should be soft and creamy with firm pieces of egg throughout. If over cooked, scrambled eggs will weep liquid because of the tightening of the proteins in the egg.
Add anything you like to scrambled eggs. Additions such as fresh herbs, smoked salmon, aged cheddar cheese, caviar, salmon roe, sour cream, blue cheese, truffle slices and seasonings should be stirred through just before serving.

frying

Heat 2 teaspoons of oil in a small frypan over medium heat. Break egg shell and gently slip egg into pan. Cook for 1–2 minutes or until egg is cooked to your liking.

duck egg

free-range hen egg

quail egg

soft-boiled egg

essential for eggs – hot buttered toast

poached egg

scrambled eggs

STEP ONE
Place butter and oil in a 23cm (9 inch) non-stick frypan over low heat and cook until butter has melted. Add onions to pan.

caramelised onion frittata

1 tablespoon butter
1 tablespoon oil
3 onions, sliced
8 eggs
¾ cup (6 fl oz) cream or milk
cracked black pepper
½ cup grated aged cheddar cheese
1 tablespoon thyme leaves

variations

PUMPKIN FRITTATA
Add ½ cup mashed pumpkin or sweet potato when whisking eggs.

BLUE CHEESE AND POTATO FRITTATA
When onions have cooked in the pan, sprinkle 1 cup cooked cubed potato over them. Pour in egg mixture and sprinkle blue cheese instead of cheddar over eggs.

ANTIPASTO FRITTATA
After adding eggs to the pan, top them with char grilled antipasto vegetables such as capsicum (red or green pepper), eggplant (aubergine) and zucchini (courgette). Sprinkle frittata with cheddar and continue with steps three and four.

STEP TWO
Cook onions, stirring occasionally, for 10–15 minutes or until onions are golden brown, soft and caramelised.

STEP THREE
Place eggs, cream and pepper in a bowl and whisk to combine. Pour egg mixture over onions in frypan and sprinkle with cheese and thyme. Cook frittata for 5–6 minutes or until it is almost set.

STEP FOUR
To finish cooking, place frittata under a preheated hot grill for 1 minute. Cut it into wedges and serve on hot buttered toast or with a spicy chutney. Serves 4 to 6.

caramelised onion frittata

asparagus and poached eggs with brown butter   bacon and egg pie

roast pumpkin and soft quail egg salad

angel food cake

asparagus and poached eggs with brown butter

85g (2¾ oz) butter
1 tablespoon sage leaves
500g (1 lb) fresh asparagus
4 eggs
parmesan cheese shavings
cracked black pepper

Place butter and sage in a saucepan over low heat, allow to bubble until they turn golden brown and keep warm. Trim ends from asparagus and steam until tender. While asparagus is steaming have a frypan full of simmering water to poach the eggs (see page 10).
Place eggs in simmering water one at a time and poach for 3–4 minutes or until whites are firm and yolks are soft. Place asparagus on warmed serving plates. Remove eggs from frypan with a slotted spoon and place on top of asparagus. Top with the browned butter, parmesan shavings and lots of cracked pepper. Serve immediately. Serves 4.

bacon and egg pie

1 quantity or 250g (8 oz) shortcrust pastry*
filling
6 eggs
1 cup (8 fl oz) milk
4 rashers bacon, chopped
⅓ cup grated aged cheddar cheese
2 tablespoons chopped chives
1 tablespoon chopped dill
2 teaspoons Dijon mustard
cracked black pepper
6 thin rashers bacon, rind removed

Roll out pastry on a lightly floured surface until it's 3mm (⅛ inch) thick. Place pastry in a 25cm (10 inch) pie dish and trim edges. Refrigerate for 30 minutes. Prick base of pastry and line with non-stick baking paper. Fill shell with baking weights or rice and bake at 180°C (350°F) for 5 minutes. Remove weights and paper, and cook for a further 5 minutes. (This process keeps the pastry crisp when adding wet ingredients to the pastry shell.)
Place eggs and milk in a bowl and whisk to combine. Add bacon, cheddar, chives, dill, mustard and pepper and mix to combine. Pour mixture into pastry shell, top with thin bacon rashers and bake at 160°C (315°F) for 35–45 minutes or until pie is set. Serve in hot or cold wedges with a peppery rocket (arugula) salad. Serves 6.

roast pumpkin and soft quail egg salad

500g (1 lb) Japanese* or sweet pumpkin, sliced
olive oil
cracked black pepper
½ cup marinated olives
200g (6½ oz) marinated feta cheese
3 tablespoons oregano leaves
150g (5 oz) baby rocket (arugula)
8 soft-boiled quail eggs
balsamic vinegar

Place pumpkin in a baking dish. Drizzle with olive oil and pepper, and bake at 180°C (350°F) for 35 minutes or until pumpkin is golden and soft. Allow to cool.
Toss olives, feta, oregano and rocket (arugula) in a bowl. Place salad on serving plates with pumpkin, top with quail eggs, and dress with a splash of balsamic vinegar and olive oil. Serves 4.

angel food cake

1 cup flour
1½ cups sugar
12 egg whites
½ teaspoon cream of tartar
2 teaspoons grated lemon rind
½ teaspoon vanilla extract
berries to serve

Sift flour and half the sugar into a bowl and set aside. Place egg whites and cream of tartar in a bowl and beat until soft peaks form. Gradually add remaining sugar to egg whites and beat until egg whites are thick and glossy.
Fold lemon rind, vanilla and flour mixture into egg whites. Pour mixture into a non-greased 23cm (9 inch) angel food cake tin and bake at 190°C (375°F) for 30 minutes or until cake is cooked when tested with a skewer. Invert tin and allow cake to cool. Run a knife around edges of tin to release cake. Serve with mixed berries. Serves 8.

pasta

basics

cooking fresh pasta

Fresh pasta needs less water than dried pasta. To cook fresh pasta, have a large saucepan of rapidly boiling water ready. Make sure you have enough boiling water for the pasta to cook in. Add a little oil to the water, so the pasta doesn't stick together. Add pasta to pan, ensure the water stays boiling and stir slowly for 10 seconds to separate the pasta. Boil pasta for 2–4 minutes (time depends on the type of pasta you are using) or until it is al dente.

cooking dried pasta

The most common mistake when cooking dried pasta is not having enough boiling water. Have a large saucepan of rapidly boiling water ready. Add a little oil and the pasta to the pan, and stir for 20 seconds to separate the pasta. Boil for 10–14 minutes. (Cooking time varies depending on the shape of pasta as well as the type of the flours used in the pasta.) Cook pasta until it is al dente.

al dente

Al dente means 'to the tooth'. When it's cooked, pasta should be soft but still firm when you bite into it. The easiest way to tell whether pasta is al dente is to remove a piece from the saucepan and test it between your teeth. The pasta should have some texture when you bite into it, but it should not be dry and hard in the middle.

drying fresh pasta

To dry fresh pasta, hang it over a suspended wooden spoon or a clean broom handle in a dry, airy place for 1–2 hours (time depends on the weather). Leave it hanging until it's dry and hard. Store pasta in airtight containers. Alternatively, fresh pasta can be frozen in airtight plastic bags or containers for up to 6 months. See glossary (page 187) for recipe for fresh pasta.

draining cooked pasta

To drain cooked pasta, pour it into a colander and shake colander to remove excess water. If you are serving it hot, use pasta immediately and do not rinse it. If you are serving it cold, rinse pasta under warm and then cold water. You can also refrigerate pasta and use it within 3 days.

herb fettuccine

chilli linguine

pasta machine

cracked pepper linguine

drying pappardelle

boiling pasta

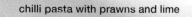

chilli pasta with prawns and lime

pasta with roast sweet potato and feta

roast vegetable lasagne

chilli pasta with prawns and lime

750g (1¹/₂ lb) medium green (raw) prawns, peeled
1 tablespoon olive oil
2 teaspoons cracked pepper
1 tablespoon chopped coriander
500g (1 lb) chilli pasta
250g (8 oz) fresh asparagus, trimmed
4 limes, halved
125g (4 oz) baby English spinach leaves
¹/₄ cup basil leaves
olive oil to serve
cracked black pepper

Place prawns, oil, pepper and coriander in a bowl and toss to combine. Place pasta in a saucepan of boiling water and cook until al dente.
Drain pasta and keep it warm. Boil or steam asparagus until tender, and chop into 5cm (2 inch) pieces.
Place prawns and limes on a hot char grill or barbecue and cook for 1 minute on each side or until tender.
Toss prawns with chilli pasta, asparagus, spinach and basil. Squeeze juice from the sweet grilled limes over pasta and top with a drizzle of olive oil and cracked black pepper. Serve immediately. Serves 4.

pasta with roast sweet potato and feta

750g (1¹/₂ lb) sweet potato
salt
oil
3 leeks, chopped
1 tablespoon fresh rosemary
500g (1 lb) pasta of your choice
2 tablespoons butter
185g (6 oz) marinated feta cheese, chopped
250g (8 oz) baby English spinach leaves
cracked black pepper
grated pecorino or parmesan cheese

Peel and chop sweet potato and place chunks in a baking dish with a little oil and salt. Bake at 200°C (400°F) for 30 minutes or until sweet potato is soft and brown.
Place oil in a frypan over medium heat. Add leeks and rosemary to oil and cook for 7 minutes or until leeks are golden and soft. Place pasta in a saucepan of boiling water and cook until al dente. Drain pasta and place in a large warmed bowl. Add sweet potato, leek mixture, butter and feta, and toss to combine.
Place piles of spinach on warmed serving plates and top with pasta, pepper and pecorino. Serves 4.

roast vegetable lasagne

2 eggplants (aubergines), sliced
salt
olive oil
250g (8 oz) English spinach leaves
3 large sheets fresh pasta, lightly cooked
12 Roma tomatoes, sliced
1 cup basil leaves
1 cup oregano leaves
1 cup shaved parmesan cheese
1 cup grated mozzarella cheese
extra oregano leaves

Place eggplant (aubergine) in a colander and sprinkle with salt. Allow slices to drain for 30 minutes and then rinse and pat dry. Brush slices with olive oil. Pan fry or char grill until slices are golden on both sides. Set aside. Place spinach in boiling water for 10 seconds to blanch, and then drain well. Line the base of an 18 x 28cm (7 x 11 inch) baking tray with non-stick baking paper. Place a layer of pasta in the baking tray and top pasta with slices of tomato, basil, oregano, eggplant (aubergine) and spinach. Sprinkle with parmesan and mozzarella. Repeat layers and top the cheese with extra oregano leaves. Bake lasagne in a preheated 180°C (350°F) oven for 40 minutes or until it is cooked through. Serves 6.

pasta with roast tomato sauce

24 Roma tomatoes,* halved
6 cloves garlic
2 tablespoons olive oil
1 tablespoon oregano leaves
2 teaspoons olive oil, extra
2 onions, chopped
1 tablespoon basil leaves
500g (1 lb) pasta of your choice
cracked black pepper
parmesan cheese shavings

Place tomatoes, garlic, oil and oregano in a baking dish and toss to combine. Bake at 160°C (315°F) for 45 minutes or until tomatoes are soft.
Place tomato mixture in a food processor and process until tomatoes are finely chopped. Heat extra oil in a saucepan over medium heat and add onions. Sauté for 5 minutes or until onions are golden.
Add tomato mixture and basil to onions and cook for 5 minutes or until sauce is heated through. Cook pasta in a saucepan of rapidly boiling water until al dente, and drain. Place pasta in a serving dish and top with tomato sauce. Sprinkle well with pepper and parmesan. Serves 4.

pasta with roast tomato sauce

angel hair pasta with tuna

500g (1 lb) fresh angel hair pasta*
120g (4 oz) rocket (arugula), roughly chopped
350g (11¼ oz) sashimi tuna,* thinly sliced
½ cup parmesan cheese shavings
2–3 tablespoons chilli oil*
cracked black pepper
lime wedges

Place pasta in a large saucepan of boiling water and cook until al dente. Drain and, while it is hot, toss pasta with rocket (arugula), tuna, parmesan, chilli oil and pepper. To serve, pile pasta on to plates and top with a squeeze of lime. Serves 4.

pasta with greens

500g (1 lb) pappardelle or wide fettuccine
1 tablespoon olive or basil oil*
2 cloves garlic, crushed
85g (2¾ oz) baby English spinach leaves
85g (2¾ oz) baby beet (beetroot) tops
85g (2¾ oz) rocket (arugula)
185g (6 oz) firm goats' cheese, crumbled
cracked black pepper
baby capers

Place pasta in a saucepan of rapidly boiling water and cook until al dente. Drain and keep pasta warm.
Heat oil in a saucepan over medium heat. Add garlic and cook until golden. Remove oil from heat. Place greens in a bowl and toss hot oil through greens.
Place pasta in serving bowls and top with greens, goats' cheese, pepper and capers. Serves 4.

pasta with baby leeks

2 tablespoons olive oil
8 baby leeks, trimmed
3 tablespoons marjoram leaves
1 tablespoon thyme leaves
500g (1lb) herb fettuccine
2 large ripe tomatoes, sliced
200g (6½ oz) smoked mozzarella cheese, sliced
cracked black pepper

Heat oil in a frypan over low heat. Add leeks, marjoram and thyme, and cook for 8 minutes or until leeks are golden and soft. Place pasta in a saucepan of boiling water and cook until al dente. Pile pasta onto serving plates and top with leek mixture, tomatoes, mozzarella and pepper. Place pasta under a hot grill for 1 minute or until mozzarella is melted and golden. Serve with wood fired bread. Serves 4.

spaghetti with grilled chicken and asparagus

500g (1 lb) spaghetti
3 chicken breast fillets
olive oil
300g (10 oz) fresh asparagus
2 red capsicums (peppers), quartered
dressing
3 tablespoons lemon juice
1 tablespoon seeded mustard
2 tablespoons olive oil
1 tablespoon dill leaves

Place spaghetti in a saucepan of rapidly boiling water and cook until al dente. Drain and keep pasta warm.
Brush chicken breasts with a little oil and place on a hot char grill or barbecue, or in a frypan. Cook for 2–3 minutes on each side or until chicken is cooked through. Blanch* asparagus in boiling water until bright green. Brush capsicums (peppers) and asparagus with oil and place on grill with chicken. Cook for a further 2 minutes.
To serve, place spaghetti in serving bowls. Slice chicken and capsicums (peppers) and place on top of spaghetti with asparagus. Combine dressing ingredients with a whisk and pour over pasta. Serve immediately. Serves 4.

pepper linguini with asian herbs

500g (1 lb) pepper linguini
½ cup Thai basil* leaves
¼ cup Vietnamese mint* leaves
2 green chillies, chopped
4 tablespoons salt-reduced soy sauce
2 tablespoons brown sugar
1 tablespoon kaffir lime* juice
2 tablespoons mirin* or sweet white cooking wine
steamed baby bok choy

Place linguini in a saucepan of boiling water and cook for 3 minutes or until al dente. Drain. Toss basil and mint through linguini. Combine chillies, soy sauce, sugar, lime juice and mirin and pour over pasta. Toss to combine.
Place linguini on serving plates and serve with steamed baby bok choy. Serves 4.

angel hair pasta with tuna

pasta with baby leeks

pasta with greens

spaghetti with grilled chicken and asparagus

pepper linguini with asian herbs

pappardelle with fennel and olives

salmon and wasabi ravioli with kaffir lime sauce

pappardelle with fennel and olives

2 red onions, chopped
2 baby fennel, sliced
2 tablespoons olive oil
¾ cup (6 fl oz) white wine
375g (12 oz) pappardelle
¼ cup basil leaves
1 cup olives
10 caper berries or capers
6 anchovies, chopped
parmesan cheese shavings

Place onions and fennel in a baking dish and toss with olive oil to coat. Add wine and bake at 200ºC (400ºF) for 30 minutes or until fennel is soft. Place pappardelle in a large saucepan of boiling water and cook until al dente. Drain pasta.
Toss hot pappardelle with fennel mixture, basil, olives, caper berries or capers and anchovies. Serve with shavings of parmesan cheese and lots of cracked pepper. Serves 4.

salmon and wasabi ravioli with kaffir lime sauce

1 quantity or 250g (8 oz) fresh pasta* or 40 wonton wrappers
filling
300g (10 oz) salmon fillet
⅓ cup crème fraîche or sour cream
125g (4 oz) ricotta cheese
wasabi* to taste (about ½ teaspoon)
1 tablespoon chopped dill
cracked pepper
kaffir lime sauce
1 cup (8 fl oz) fish or vegetable stock
6 kaffir lime* leaves, shredded
¾ cup (6 fl oz) cream

Cut pasta into 10cm (4 inch) squares and set aside. To make filling, cut salmon into slices 2cm (¾ inch) thick. Place salmon, crème fraîche, ricotta, wasabi, dill and pepper in a bowl and mix to combine. Place spoonfuls of filling on pasta squares or wonton wrappers and top with another pasta square or wonton wrapper. Press squares firmly around edges to seal.
To make sauce, place stock, lime leaves and cream in a saucepan and simmer gently until reduced by half.
To cook ravioli, place it in a large saucepan of boiling water and cook for 6–8 minutes or until pasta is al dente. Drain. Place ravioli in serving bowls and spoon sauce over it. Top with cracked pepper. Serves 4 to 6.

fettuccine with lemon swordfish

500g (1 lb) fettuccine
2 tablespoons olive oil
1 tablespoon grated lemon rind
1 clove garlic, crushed
1 red chilli, chopped
2 tablespoons lemon thyme leaves
2 tablespoons butter
350g (11¼ oz) swordfish, cubed
1 lemon, thinly sliced
cracked black pepper
grated parmesan cheese

Place fettuccine in a saucepan of boiling water and cook until al dente. Drain and keep pasta warm.
While pasta is cooking, heat oil in a saucepan over medium heat. Add lemon rind, garlic, chilli and thyme and cook for 3 minutes. Keep warm.
Heat butter in a frypan over medium heat. Add swordfish to pan and cook for 2–3 minutes or until fish is golden and tender.
Remove swordfish from pan and keep it warm. Add lemon slices to pan and fry for 2 minutes on each side or until golden.
Toss swordfish and spice mixture through fettuccine and serve in deep bowls. Top pasta with parmesan and pepper. Serve with fried lemon slices on the side. Serves 4.

fettuccine with fried basil, garlic and capers

500g (1 lb) fettuccine
3 tablespoons fruity olive oil
¼ cup basil leaves
5 cloves garlic, crushed
2 tablespoons baby capers
2 tablespoons lemon juice
4 bocconcini,* sliced
parmesan cheese shavings
cracked black pepper

Place fettuccine in a large saucepan of boiling water and cook until al dente. Drain and keep pasta warm.
Place oil in a frypan over medium heat. Add basil, garlic and capers and fry until garlic is golden and basil is crisp. Add lemon juice and toss basil mixture through pasta.
Place slices of bocconcini on serving plates.
Top with pasta and shavings of parmesan and a generous sprinkling of cracked black pepper. Serve immediately. Serves 4 to 6.

fettuccine with lemon swordfish   fettuccine with fried basil, garlic and capers

rice

basics

In many cultures rice symbolises fertility and life – consequently we have the age-old tradition of throwing rice at weddings. In some circles, spilling or upsetting a bowl of rice is considered to be very bad luck, so be careful when tipping the contents of those rice bags into airtight containers for storage. For the fact file, rice is the most highly consumed food in the world!

varieties or types

short and medium grain

Short- and medium-grain rice have traditionally been used by the English for puddings, although the Japanese use them for everyday sushi, the Spanish for paella and the Chinese eat medium-grain rice at almost every meal. The plump, moist grains stick together when cooked properly, making them easy to eat with chopsticks.

brown

Brown rice comes in long- and short-grain varieties. The outer husk or bran of brown rice is not polished away as it is for white rice. Therefore, brown rice is nutritionally superior to white rice and has a slightly nutty taste. Brown rice takes approximately 40 minutes to cook as the water has to penetrate the bran.

arborio

Arborio (or Italian) rice takes its name from a village in the Piedmont region of northern Italy. This round, short-grain rice is used for risotto. It releases some of its starch when cooked, making a creamy savoury rice dish. Other varieties used for risotto include violone and carnaroli.

long grain

Long-grain rice separates into individual grains when cooked. Jasmine and basmati rice are both long-grain varieties.

wild

Wild rice is not really a rice but the grain from a water grass native to North America. It has a distinctive nutty flavour with a chewy texture and comes with a fairly hefty price tag. You can mix it with other varieties of rice.

glutinous

Glutinous rice comes in plump, opaque grains, which can be either white or black, or short or long. These grains become sticky and sweet when cooked. It is necessary to soak glutinous rice overnight if you are steaming it. It can be used unsoaked if you are cooking it by the absorption method. Predominantly used in sweets, glutinous rice is also the staple rice of some Asian countries.

arborio rice

brown rice

short-grain rice

long-grain, jasmine and basmati rice

white and black glutinous rice

wild rice

basic risotto

4–4½ cups (32–36 fl oz) vegetable
or chicken stock
1 cup (8 fl oz) dry white wine
1 tablespoon olive oil
1 tablespoon butter

1 onion, finely chopped
2 cups arborio rice
½ cup shaved or grated parmesan
cheese
cracked black pepper

STEP ONE
Place stock and wine in
a saucepan over
medium heat and bring
to a very slow simmer.
Place olive oil and
butter in a heavy-based
saucepan over medium
heat. Add onion to oil
and butter, and cook
until soft.

STEP TWO
Add rice to oil,
butter and onion
and cook, stirring,
for 1 minute or until
rice is translucent.

STEP THREE
Slowly add 1 cup of
stock to rice and stir
constantly until liquid
has been absorbed.
Repeat, only adding
more stock after liquid
has been absorbed.
Continue adding stock
until rice is soft and
risotto is creamy. If you
need more liquid, heat
extra stock or water.
Risotto should have
firm but tender grains
of rice.

STEP FOUR
When rice is almost
cooked, stir through
parmesan and
pepper. Serve
risotto in deep
bowls on a bed of
steamed greens
generously
sprinkled with
cracked black
pepper. Serves 4.

basic risotto

sweet potato and chicken risotto

350g (11¼ oz) sweet potato, peeled and chopped
4–4½ cups (32–36 fl oz) chicken stock
1 cup (8 fl oz) dry white wine
1 tablespoon olive oil
1 tablespoon butter
2 leeks, chopped
2 chicken breast fillets, chopped
2 cups arborio rice
⅓ cup shaved or grated parmesan cheese
2 tablespoons butter
cracked black pepper

Place sweet potato in a greased baking dish and bake at 180ºC (350ºF) for 25 minutes or until crisp. Place stock and wine in a saucepan and heat to a slow simmer. Place oil and butter in a heavy-based saucepan over medium heat. Add leek and cook until soft and golden. Add chicken to pan and cook for 4 minutes or until browned. Remove chicken mixture from pan using a slotted spoon and set aside.
Add rice to pan and cook in pan juices until rice is translucent. Add stock a cup at a time to rice and stir continuously. Just before risotto is cooked, add chicken mixture and parmesan and stir well. Mash half the sweet potato with butter and add it to risotto.
To serve, place risotto on a serving plate and top with remaining roasted sweet potato. Add cracked black pepper. Serves 4.

saffron porcini risotto cakes

25g (¾ oz) dry porcini mushrooms*
2 cups (16 fl oz) warm water
¼ teaspoon saffron* threads
¼ cup (2 fl oz) water
2 cups (16 fl oz) vegetable stock
1 cup (8 fl oz) dry white wine
2 tablespoons oil
2 leeks, chopped
2 cups arborio rice
1 tablespoon chopped lemon thyme
½ cup grated parmesan cheese
1 teaspoon cracked black pepper
flour to coat
oil for shallow frying

Place porcini mushrooms in warm water and allow them to soak for 30 minutes. Squeeze water from porcini and filter soaking water through a fine sieve lined with paper. Place saffron in water and stand for 5 minutes. Place porcini liquid, saffron mixture, stock and wine in a saucepan and

bring to a slow, steady simmer. Place oil in a heavy-based saucepan over medium heat. Add leeks to pan and cook for 5 minutes or until soft and golden. Add rice to pan and cook, stirring until rice is translucent. Add stock mixture 1 cup at a time as described on page 36. Continue cooking until risotto is almost cooked. Add chopped porcini, thyme, parmesan and pepper, and continue cooking until rice is firm but tender. Allow risotto to cool for 10 minutes. Shape risotto into patties and toss in flour. Shallow fry cakes in hot oil. Drain and serve. Serves 6.

miso and shiitake risotto

3 tablespoons miso*
4 cups water
½ cup cooking sake* or wine
½ cup cooking sherry
1 teaspoon sesame oil
1 tablespoon peanut oil
2 red chillies, chopped
150g (5 oz) shiitake mushrooms,* sliced
2 cups arborio rice
1 tablespoon chopped Vietnamese mint*
2 tablespoons chopped chives
steamed bok choy to serve
cracked black pepper

Place miso, water, sake and sherry in a saucepan and allow to simmer slowly. Place oils in a heavy-based saucepan over medium heat. Add chillies and cook for 1 minute. Add shiitake mushrooms and cook for 2 minutes or until mushrooms are soft. Remove mushrooms with a slotted spoon and set aside.
Add rice to pan and cook, stirring, until rice is translucent. Add 1 cup of liquid at a time to rice and stir until liquid is absorbed. Repeat until rice is almost tender. Add shiitake mushrooms, mint and chives.
To serve, place steamed bok choy on a serving plate, top with risotto and sprinkle with pepper. Serves 4.

tomato and fennel risotto

6 Roma* tomatoes
olive oil
440g (14 oz) can peeled tomatoes, mashed
2 cups (16 fl oz) beef stock
1 cup (8 fl oz) red wine
2 tablespoons olive oil, extra
2 onions, chopped
2 cloves garlic, crushed
3 baby fennel, sliced
2 cups arborio rice
⅓ cup grated mature firm goats' cheese
cracked black pepper

sweet potato and chicken risotto

miso and shiitake risotto

saffron porcini risotto cakes

tomato and fennel risotto

Place tomatoes on a baking tray and drizzle olive oil and pepper over them. Bake at 160°C (315°F) for 30 minutes. Place canned tomatoes, stock and wine in a saucepan and bring to a steady simmer.

Place extra oil in a heavy-based saucepan over medium heat. Add onions and garlic to pan and cook for 3 minutes or until soft. Add fennel to pan and cook for 8–10 minutes or until soft.

Add rice to pan and cook, stirring, until rice is translucent. Add stock mixture 1 cup at a time, stirring until liquid has been absorbed. Repeat until liquid has been used or until rice is tender but firm. Stir in cheese and pepper. Place risotto in shallow plates, and serve with roasted tomatoes and thinly sliced rare beef. Serves 6.

coconut rice with green chilli

2 cups short- or long-grain white rice
2 cups (16 fl oz) water
1 cup (8 fl oz) coconut cream
2 green chillies, seeded and chopped
2 tablespoons coriander leaves
6 banana leaves

Wash rice well and place in a saucepan with water and coconut cream. Place saucepan over high heat and allow liquid to boil. Boil for 8 minutes or until tunnels form in rice and liquid has almost been absorbed. Remove from heat. Stir chillies and coriander through rice and pile mixture onto banana leaves. Fold over leaves to encase rice. Put parcels in bamboo steamers* and steam for 5 minutes. Serve with coconut chicken curry (see page 120). Serves 6.

lemon and basil pilaf

1 tablespoon oil
2 onions, chopped
2 cloves garlic, crushed
1 tablespoon grated lemon rind
2 cups long-grain rice
4½ cups (36 fl oz) vegetable stock
½ cup basil leaves
cracked black pepper
butter

Place oil in a saucepan over medium heat. Add onion and garlic to oil and cook for 4 minutes or until onion and garlic are golden. Add lemon rind and rice to pan, and cook for 3 minutes or until rice is translucent.

Add stock and basil to rice mixture and allow to simmer for 15 minutes or until stock is absorbed. Sprinkle well with cracked pepper and stir a little butter through mixture. Serve with grilled fish and lemon wedges. Serves 4 to 6.

rice in lotus leaves

1 tablespoon oil
3 shallots, chopped
2 teaspoons grated ginger
1 chicken breast fillet, finely chopped
1 cup chopped Chinese barbecue duck*
½ cup chopped shiitake mushrooms*
3 tablespoons soy sauce
2 teaspoons sugar
4 cups cooked long-grain or glutinous rice
4 dried lotus leaves

Heat oil in a wok over high heat. Add shallots and ginger and cook for 2 minutes. Add chicken, duck and mushrooms to wok and cook for a further 4 minutes. Add soy sauce, sugar and rice to wok and stir well. Soak lotus leaves in water until soft. Dry leaves. Place rice in lotus leaves and fold them over to form a parcel. Place parcels in bamboo steamers* and steam for 15 minutes. Serves 4.

soy rice and chicken

2 chicken breasts on the bone
4 tablespoons light soy sauce
2 tablespoons sweet white wine
1 tablespoon shredded ginger
2½ cups short- or long-grain white rice
3¾ cups (30 fl oz) cold water
6 shallots, chopped
125g (4 oz) oyster mushrooms*
1 teaspoon cornflour (cornstarch)

Chop chicken into small pieces and place in a bowl with soy sauce, wine and ginger. Allow chicken to marinate for 30 minutes.

Wash rice well under cold water. Place in a large saucepan and pour cold water over rice. Bring water to boil and cook rice for 5 minutes. Reduce heat to low. Drain chicken from marinade and reserve marinade.

Place chicken, shallots and mushrooms on top of rice. Cover pan tightly and cook for a further 15 minutes or until chicken is tender.

Place reserved marinade in a saucepan and bring to boil. Mix cornflour (cornstarch) with a little water to form a smooth paste. Whisk into marinade and cook for 1 minute. Place rice and chicken mixture in serving bowls and top with sauce. Serves 4.

coconut rice with green chilli

rice in lotus leaves

lemon and basil pilaf

soy rice and chicken

noodles

basics

dried rice

Dried rice noodles range in thickness from thin threads (vermicelli) to flat ribbons or rice sticks. Vermicelli noodles need to be cooked in boiling water for 2 minutes. Thicker noodles need 3–4 minutes before draining. Be sure to test noodles frequently as they should be firm, especially if you are adding them to a stir fry or cooking them further in a recipe.

somen

Somen noodles are fine white Japanese noodles made from wheat and water or egg yolk. These noodles are often cooked lightly in boiling water and served cold with a dipping sauce or in soups.

fresh rice

Fresh rice noodles come in a variety of widths and are located in the refrigerated section of Asian and some general supermarkets. Keep them for only a few days in the refrigerator. To prepare, soak noodles in hot to boiling water for 1 minute, separating them gently with a fork. Drain and use as recipe requires.

shanghai

Shanghai noodles are soft, flattish, fresh wheat noodles. You'll find them in the refrigerated section of Asian supermarkets. They have a firm texture when cooked and are used in Chinese soups and stir fries.

hokkien

Hokkien noodles are round, yellow wheat noodles available from the refrigerated section of Asian and general supermarkets. Place noodles in a bowl and cover them with hot to boiling water. Soak for 1–2 minutes or until noodles have softened. Drain noodles and use as recipe requires.

cellophane

Cellophane noodles or bean starch noodles are made from the starch of mung beans and come as vermicelli or as flat, wide noodles. They are difficult to cut and separate when dried, so buy them in small bundles if possible. They need to be soaked in boiling water for 10 minutes or until soft, and then drained. (This method allows you to cut the noodles into shorter lengths.) You can also deep fry them straight from the packet.

soba

Soba noodles are Japanese noodles made from buckwheat. Sometimes wheat flour is added as well as flavourings such as green tea, shiso leaves and black sesame seeds.

fresh egg

Fresh egg noodles are available in many different thicknesses and shapes in Asian supermarkets. Boil them in water for 2 minutes before adding to a stir fry.

ramen

Ramen noodles are used extensively in Japan, although they are Chinese in origin. They can be purchased fresh but are much more readily available dried. They are used in Japanese noodle soups. The fresh noodles need to be boiled until they are tender before being added to a soup. Most dried ramen noodles are instant and only need boiling water poured over them to be cooked.

dried egg

Dried egg noodles are available in a variety of thicknesses and need to be boiled until just tender. Drain and add to recipe as required.

udon

Udon noodles are soft, creamy, buff-coloured Japanese wheat flour noodles. They are usually boiled in stock or soup broth and served as an informal, warming snack. They are readily available dried in bundles and you can also find them fresh in some Asian supermarkets.

hokkien noodles

fresh rice noodles

dried rice noodles

shanghai noodles

45

noodles

cellophane noodles

fresh egg noodles

dried egg noodles

dried ramen noodles

fresh ramen noodles

dried somen noodles

fresh somen noodles

fresh udon noodles

dried udon noodles

buckwheat soba noodles

barbecue duck and ramen soup   rare beef and cellophane noodle salad

shanghai noodle stir fry

barbecue duck and ramen soup

3 cups (24 fl oz) chicken stock
5 cups (40 fl oz) water
8 slices ginger or galangal*
2 red chillies, halved and seeded
2 tablespoons lime or lemon juice
2 stalks lemon grass*
2 coriander roots
1 Chinese barbecue duck,* flesh removed and chopped
4 shallots, chopped
200g (6½ oz) fresh or 150g (5 oz) dried ramen noodles
bean sprouts, chilli and coriander to garnish

Place stock and water in a saucepan and heat until liquid is simmering. Continue simmering and add galangal, chillies and lime juice. Bruise lemon grass and coriander with the back of a cleaver to release flavours and add to saucepan. Allow liquid to simmer for 20 minutes.
Strain liquid, return to saucepan and return to heat with duck and shallots. Boil ramen noodles in a separate saucepan for 3–5 minutes or until tender, and drain. Add noodles to soup and simmer for 5 minutes. Ladle soup and noodles into bowls and garnish with bean sprouts, chilli strips and coriander. Serves 4 to 6.

rare beef and cellophane noodle salad

500g (1 lb) thick rump steak
200g (6½ oz) cellophane noodles
1 green mango, peeled
½ cup Thai basil* leaves
½ cup mint leaves
⅓ cup coriander leaves
dressing
4 tablespoons lime juice
3 tablespoons soy sauce
2 tablespoons brown sugar
1 green chilli, seeded and chopped

Heat a grill or frypan on high heat for 2 minutes. Place steak in pan and cook for 1–2 minutes on each side or until juices are sealed in and meat is cooked medium rare. Set aside.
Place noodles in boiling water and allow to stand for 5 minutes before draining. Chop mango finely and combine with noodles, basil, mint and coriander.
To make dressing, place lime juice, soy sauce, sugar and chilli in a bowl and mix to combine.
Slice steak thinly, and toss with noodle mixture and dressing. To serve, pile salad onto serving plates. Serves 4.

shanghai noodle stir fry

500g (1 lb) fresh thick Shanghai noodles
2 teaspoons sesame oil
1 tablespoon oil
4 shallots, chopped
½ Chinese cabbage, shredded
1 chicken breast, thinly sliced
250g (8 oz) lean pork loin, thinly sliced
150g (5 oz) bok choy, chopped
3 tablespoons soy sauce
1 tablespoon hoi sin sauce*

Place noodles in a wok or saucepan of boiling water and allow to boil for 5 minutes. Drain and rinse in cold water. Heat oils in a wok. Add shallots and cook for 1 minute. Add noodles and stir fry for 4 minutes. Add remaining ingredients and cook for 5–7 minutes or until they are cooked through. Serve with chilli sauce. Serves 4.

chilled soba noodle salad

300g (10 oz) dried buckwheat soba noodles
1 cucumber, chopped
1 tablespoon shredded ginger
2 tablespoons black sesame seeds
4 shallots, chopped
125g (4 oz) sashimi tuna,* thinly sliced
dressing
4 tablespoons Japanese soy sauce
4 tablespoons mirin*
wasabi* to taste

Place noodles in a large saucepan of boiling water. When water returns to boil, add 1 cup (8 fl oz) cold water and bring to boil again. Cook for 8 minutes or until noodles are tender. Rinse noodles under cold water and drain well. Place noodles in refrigerator to cool. Toss cold noodles with cucumber, ginger, sesame seeds and shallots. Place noodles on serving plates and top with tuna.
To make dressing, place soy sauce, mirin and wasabi in a bowl and whisk to combine. Serve dressing in small bowls next to each salad. Serves 4 to 6.

chilled soba noodle salad

rice noodle pancakes

udon noodles in miso broth   hokkien noodles with seared scallops

somen noodles with chilli and lime dipping sauce

thai rice noodles

egg noodles with chinese barbecue pork

rice noodle pancakes

300g (10 oz) fresh thin rice noodles
2 green chillies, seeded and chopped
2 teaspoons shredded ginger
2 tablespoons chopped coriander
2 tablespoons sesame seeds
oil for shallow frying
350g (11¼ oz) pork fillet, sliced very thinly
2 tablespoons soy sauce
2 teaspoons grated lime rind
hoi sin sauce*

Place noodles in a bowl, pour boiling water over them,
allow to stand for 3 minutes and then drain well. Place
noodles on absorbent paper to drain away any excess
water.
Combine noodles with chillies, ginger, coriander and
sesame seeds. Heat 1 cm (½ inch) of oil in a frypan over
medium heat. Place spoonfuls of noodle mixture in frypan
and flatten them with a spatula. Cook pancakes for 2–3
minutes on each side or until they are golden and crisp.
Drain pancakes on absorbent kitchen paper and repeat the
process with remaining mixture.
Place pork, soy sauce and lime rind in a shallow dish and
marinate for 10 minutes. Char grill pork on a hot preheated
grill for 3–4 minutes or until it is cooked medium.
To serve, place pancakes in a stack on a serving plate. Top
with very thin slices of pork and a drizzle of hoi sin sauce.
Serves 6.

udon noodles in miso broth

6 cups (48 fl oz) cold water
8cm (3 inch) piece kombu (dried seaweed)
5 tablespoons dried bonito flakes*
2 tablespoons red miso*
250g (8 oz) dried udon noodles
300g fresh asparagus, trimmed and halved
150g (5 oz) firm tofu, chopped
2 shallots, chopped

Place water and kombu in a saucepan and slowly bring to
the boil. As soon as water boils, remove kombu. Remove
water from heat and add bonito flakes. Return saucepan to
heat and bring liquid to the boil. As soon as liquid boils,
remove it from heat and set aside for 1 minute. Strain liquid
through a fine sieve or muslin.
Place strained liquid in a saucepan and bring to the boil.
Add a little of the liquid to the miso and mix until smooth.
Add miso to pan. Add noodles and asparagus to pan and
boil for 6–8 minutes or until al dente. Stir tofu and shallots
through noodle mixture. Serve immediately. Serves 4 to 6.

hokkien noodles with seared scallops

350g (11¼ oz) Hokkien noodles
2 teaspoons sesame oil
8 shallots, trimmed and halved
1 tablespoon shredded ginger
200g (6½ oz) snake beans, trimmed and chopped
250g (8 oz) Chinese broccoli (gai larn), chopped
3 tablespoons oyster sauce
2 tablespoons sweet chilli sauce
12 scallops
1 tablespoon chilli oil*
lime wedges

Place noodles in a bowl and cover with boiling water. Allow
noodles to stand for 2 minutes and drain well.
Heat oil in a wok or frypan over high heat. Add shallots and
ginger and stir fry for 2 minutes. Add snake beans, Chinese
broccoli (gai larn), oyster sauce and sweet chilli sauce to
wok and cook for 2 minutes. Add noodles and cook for a
further 3 minutes or until noodles are heated through.
Place noodles in piles on warmed serving plates or in
bowls. Heat chilli oil in a wok or frypan over high heat. Add
scallops to wok and cook for 10–20 seconds on each side
or until just seared.
To serve, place scallops on top of noodles and serve with
lime wedges. Serves 4.

somen noodles with chilli and lime dipping sauce

350g (11¼ oz) dried somen noodles
12 cooked medium prawns, shelled
chilli and lime dipping sauce
1 teaspoon sesame oil
2 red chillies, seeded and chopped
2 teaspoons grated ginger
4 tablespoons soy sauce
2 tablespoons sweet sherry
3 tablespoons lime juice
2 tablespoons brown sugar

Place noodles in a saucepan of boiling water and allow to
boil for 10 minutes or until al dente. Drain and run noodles
under cold water. Chill noodles in refrigerator until cold.
To make dipping sauce, place oil in a saucepan over
medium heat. Add chillies and ginger, and sauté for
1 minute. Remove pan from heat and stir soy sauce, sherry,
lime juice and sugar through oil mixture.
To serve, place noodles and prawns on serving plates.
Spoon dipping sauce into small bowls and place one on
each plate. Serves 4.

thai rice noodles

350g (11¼ oz) fresh or 150g (5 oz) dried rice noodles
2 teaspoons oil
4 shallots, chopped
1 red chilli, seeded and chopped
1 small piece ginger, shredded
1 chicken breast fillet, chopped
12 green (raw) prawns, shelled and deveined
4 tablespoons soy sauce
2 teaspoons fish sauce*
2 tablespoons brown or palm sugar*
100g (3¼ oz) firm tofu, chopped
2 tablespoons lemon or lime juice
100g (3¼ oz) bean sprouts
2 tablespoons mint leaves
2 tablespoons basil leaves

Prepare noodles following instructions on page 44. Place oil in a wok over high heat. Add shallots, chilli and ginger and stir fry for 2 minutes. Add chicken and prawns and cook for 3 minutes or until chicken is golden.
Add soy sauce, fish sauce, sugar and noodles, and cook for 2 minutes. Add tofu, lemon juice, bean sprouts, mint and basil, and cook for 1 minute. Serve with extra lime or lemon wedges. Serves 4.

egg noodles with chinese barbecue pork

350g (11¼ oz) fresh or 200g (6½ oz) dried egg noodles
1 tablespoon sesame oil
2 onions, chopped
1 green capsicum (pepper), chopped
200g (6½ oz) bok choy
350g (11¼ oz) Chinese barbecue pork,* sliced
3 tablespoons dark soy sauce
2 tablespoons sweet white cooking wine
¼ cup (2 fl oz) chicken stock
chilli sauce for serving

Prepare noodles following instructions on page 44. Heat oil in a wok or frypan over high heat. Add onions and cook for 5 minutes or until golden. Add capsicum (pepper), bok choy and pork and stir fry for 2 minutes.
Add noodles, soy sauce, wine and stock to wok and cook for 4 minutes or until heated through. Serve in deep bowls with chilli sauce on the side. Serves 4.

noodle and asian herb soup

200g (6¼ oz) rice vermicelli
3 tablespoons Vietnamese mint*
3 tablespoons basil leaves
1 cup bean sprouts or pea shoots
6 cups (48 fl oz) chicken stock
6 kaffir lime* leaves
2 red chillies, seeded and chopped
4 slices ginger
3 chicken breast fillets

Cook vermicelli in boiling water until tender, and drain. Divide noodles between 6 serving bowls and top with mint, basil and sprouts.
Place stock, lime leaves, chillies and ginger in a saucepan and bring to boil. Add chicken and poach for 4 minutes or until chicken is cooked through. Remove chicken and shred meat. Continue to simmer stock for 5 minutes.
To serve, place shredded chicken on top of noodles and ladle hot stock mixture into bowls. Serve immediately. Serves 6.

noodle and asian herb soup

vegetables

basics

steaming

Steaming is an easy way to cook vegetables and almost all vegetables can be steamed. Steaming vegetables retains their water-soluble vitamins. Vegetables that don't take well to steaming are the starchy ones such as potatoes. When steaming, make sure that vegetables are cut into equal-sized pieces so they cook evenly. To steam vegetables, place them in a bamboo* or metal steamer, place lid on steamer and put steamer over a saucepan of boiling water. Steam is extremely hot, so be careful not to over cook vegetables. Serve vegetables soon after steaming.

mashing

Mashing or puréeing is a great way to serve a variety of vegetables including potatoes, parsnip, pumpkin and celeriac. Food processors are often used to purée vegetables, although mashing potatoes in the food processor gives them a starchy, gluey texture, so these are best done with a masher or fork. Adding milk or cream when mashing will thin the mash as well as giving it richness. Adding butter to mash also gives richness. Be sure to purchase varieties of potatoes that are good for mashing. Pepper, roast garlic, herbs and freshly ground spices are great to add to mashed or puréed vegetables. For good mashed potato, boil peeled potatoes until they are soft. Drain and put them in a warm place on the stove top to keep them hot while mashing. Add a teaspoon of butter for each large potato to be mashed. Mash potatoes with a masher or fork and add enough milk to form a smooth mash. Season with any extra flavours and serve.

roasting

A variety of vegetables can be roasted including root vegetables, onions, pumpkin and capsicums (peppers). Some vegetables (pumpkin and sweet potato) are better peeled and others (beetroot and potatoes) just need a good scrub before roasting. For even browning, place vegetables in a baking dish and drizzle oil over them. Shake the dish well to coat vegetables. For salt and rosemary potatoes, add 2 teaspoons of sea salt and 1 tablespoon of rosemary leaves. Bake at 200°C (400°F) for 45 minutes to 1 hour or until potatoes are golden.

stir frying

Stir frying is an easy and quick way to prepare vegetables. The secret to stir frying is to have the pan or wok very hot and the vegetables cut into similar-sized pieces so they cook evenly. Starchy vegetables are not suitable for stir frying. Stir-fried vegetables should be flavoured near the end of the cooking time. For simple stir-fried vegetables, heat sesame oil over high heat in a wok or frypan. Add assorted vegetables and stir fry for 3–5 minutes. Complete the dish with a squeeze of lemon and cracked black pepper. Serve immediately.

char grilling

Capsicum (pepper), zucchini (courgette), eggplant (aubergine) and fennel are just a few of the vegetables that are great for char grilling. The most important rule when char grilling is to brush the vegetables, not the char grill, with oil. Greasing the char grill will cause a lot of smoke during the cooking process. Char grill vegetables on both sides until tender. Pour a dressing over to marinate or serve vegetables with grilled or roast meat.

mashing

steaming

char grilling

stir frying

roasting

baked celeriac and blue cheese

chinese greens in oyster sauce

tomato, smoked mozzarella and oregano pizza

baked celeriac and blue cheese

500g (1 lb) celeriac, peeled and sliced
1/2 cup chopped roasted hazelnuts
3 potatoes, peeled and sliced
2 cups (16 fl oz) cream
150g (5 oz) blue cheese, crumbled
1 teaspoon caraway seeds

Layer celeriac, hazelnuts and potatoes in a greased
ovenproof dish. Pour over cream and bake in a preheated
200°C (400°F) oven for 40 minutes.
Sprinkle over cheese and caraway seeds and bake for a
further 15 minutes or until vegetables are soft and cheese is
golden. Serve with roast meat. Serves 4.

chinese greens in oyster sauce

250g (8 oz) Chinese broccoli (gai larn)
150g (5 oz) choy sum
sauce
2 teaspoons sesame oil
1 teaspoon grated ginger
3 tablespoons oyster sauce
3 tablespoons chicken stock
1 tablespoon soy sauce
2 teaspoons sugar

Cut Chinese broccoli (gai larn) and choy sum into short
lengths. Place vegetables in boiling water for 30 seconds
and then drain.
To make sauce, heat oil in a wok over high heat. Add
ginger and cook for 1 minute.
Add remaining ingredients and cook for 2 minutes. Toss
vegetables in sauce and cook for 1 minute or until heated
through. Serve immediately. Serves 4.

tomato, smoked mozzarella and oregano pizza

1 quantity pizza dough*
topping
300g (10 oz) smoked mozzarella cheese, sliced
2 green tomatoes, sliced
2 red tomatoes, sliced
2 cloves garlic, sliced
3 tablespoons oregano leaves
olive oil
1/2 cup parmesan cheese shavings

Heat 2 baking trays in a preheated 180°C (350°F) oven.
Divide pizza dough into 4 pieces and roll until they are

3mm (1/8 inch) thick. Top dough with slices of mozzarella,
and green and red tomatoes. Sprinkle garlic, oregano, oil,
and parmesan over pizzas. Slide pizzas onto preheated
baking trays and bake for 25 minutes or until crust is
golden. Serves 4.

vegetable pies

1 quantity or 250g (8 oz) shortcrust pastry*
filling
750g (1 1/2 lb) potatoes, chopped
2 tablespoons butter
1/2 cup (4 fl oz) milk
1/2 cup grated cheddar cheese
300g (10 oz) pumpkin, chopped
300g (10 oz) sweet potato, chopped
200g (6 1/2 oz) broccoli, chopped
120g (4 oz) green beans, trimmed and halved
2 tablespoons chopped basil
1/2 cup grated parmesan cheese

Roll out pastry on a lightly floured surface until it's 3mm
(1/8 inch) thick. Line 6 small pie dishes with pastry and
refrigerate until required.
Cook potatoes in a saucepan of boiling water until soft.
Drain and mash potatoes with butter and milk, and stir
through cheddar cheese.
Boil pumpkin and sweet potato until soft, and then drain
and mix with mashed potato, broccoli, beans and basil.
Spoon vegetables into pastry cases and top with
parmesan.
Bake in a preheated 200°C (400°F) oven for
30 minutes or until pies are golden. Serves 6.

rice paper rolls

12 rice paper rounds
1 cup snow pea sprouts
1/2 cup shredded carrot
1/2 cup shredded raw beetroot
125g (4 oz) enoki mushrooms*
1/4 cup mint leaves
1/4 cup Thai basil* leaves
dipping sauce
2 tablespoons lime juice
2 tablespoons chilli sauce
2 teaspoons brown sugar

Soak rice paper rounds a few at a time in warm water until
they are soft. Place a small pile of sprouts, carrot, beetroot,
mushrooms, mint and basil on each rice paper. Fold and
roll to enclose.
To make dipping sauce, combine lime juice, chilli sauce and
sugar. Serve rice paper rolls with dipping sauce. Serves 4.

vegetable pies

roast capsicum soup

sweet potato soup

spinach, lemon and lentil soup

onion and fennel soup

roast capsicum soup

5 red capsicums (peppers), quartered
1 tablespoon oil
2 cloves garlic
2 red onions, chopped
4 tomatoes, peeled and chopped
4 cups (32 fl oz) chicken stock
cracked black pepper

Place capsicum (pepper) quarters under a hot grill, skin side up, and grill until skins are black and charred. Put capsicums (peppers) in a plastic bag, seal and allow to stand for 5 minutes. Remove capsicums from bag and peel away skins.

Heat oil in a frypan over medium heat. Add garlic and onions and cook for 4 minutes or until onions are soft and golden. Add tomatoes and cook for 5 minutes or until tomatoes are very soft. Place capsicums (peppers) and tomato mixture in a blender or food processor and process until smooth.

Return mixture to saucepan and add stock. Place pan over medium heat for 5 minutes or until soup is hot. Sprinkle with cracked black pepper and serve with toast. Serves 4.

sweet potato soup

1kg (2 lb) sweet potato, peeled and chopped
2 teaspoons oil
2 tablespoons shredded ginger
2 teaspoons cumin seeds
2 red chillies, chopped
2 stalks lemon grass,* finely chopped
2 cups (16 fl oz) vegetable stock
2 cups (16 fl oz) coconut milk
1 tablespoon palm or brown sugar
1/2 cup coriander leaves

Place sweet potato in a saucepan of boiling water and cook for 5 minutes or until tender. Drain and set aside. Heat oil in a saucepan over medium heat. Add ginger, cumin seeds, chillies and lemon grass and cook for 3 minutes. Place sweet potato and spice mixture in a food processor or blender and process with a little stock until smooth. Place sweet potato mixture in a saucepan over medium heat. Add remaining stock, coconut milk and palm sugar, and stir until soup is simmering and hot. Stir through coriander and serve. Serves 4.

spinach, lemon and lentil soup

350g (11¼ oz) green lentils
1 tablespoon olive oil
3 leeks, finely chopped
4 cloves garlic, crushed
3 potatoes, peeled and chopped
3 bay leaves
4 sprigs thyme
4 sprigs oregano
4 cups (32 fl oz) vegetable stock
8 cups (64 fl oz) water
500g (1 lb) English spinach, trimmed and chopped
1/3 cup (2¾ fl oz) lemon juice

Place lentils in a bowl, cover with cold water and allow to stand for 2 hours.

Heat oil in a large saucepan over medium heat. Add leeks and garlic to pan and cook for 6 minutes or until golden and soft. Add potatoes, bay leaves, thyme, oregano, stock, water and drained lentils to pan and simmer for 40 minutes or until lentils are soft.

Add spinach and lemon juice to soup and cook for 1 minute. Serve soup with grilled Turkish bread. Serves 6.

onion and fennel soup

1 tablespoon oil
6 onions, chopped
2 tablespoons chopped thyme
1 tablespoon rosemary leaves
4 cups (32 fl oz) beef or vegetable stock
2 cups (16 fl oz) water
350g (11¼ oz) fennel, sliced
parmesan cheese shavings
cracked black pepper

Place oil in a saucepan over low heat. Add onions, thyme and rosemary to pan and cook for 10 minutes or until onions are soft and well browned. Add stock, water and fennel to pan and simmer for 8 minutes.

To serve, place soup in bowls and top with parmesan and pepper. Serves 4.

rice paper rolls

eggplant and chick pea salad

onion tart

shiitake mushroom omelette

baby spinach, cheese and olive pie

stir-fried beans with lemon and cashews

asparagus with sweet sake and ginger

sweet potato and sage tart

eggplant and chick pea salad

2 eggplants (aubergines), chopped
salt
3 tablespoons olive oil
3 cloves garlic, sliced
2 teaspoons ground coriander
1 teaspoon cardamom seeds
1 teaspoon ground cinnamon
2 cups cooked chick peas
1/2 cup chopped flat-leaf (Italian) parsley
200g (6 1/2 oz) baby English spinach leaves
dressing
1/2 cup (4 fl oz) yoghurt
2 tablespoons chopped mint
2 teaspoons honey
2 teaspoons ground cumin

Place eggplant (aubergine) chunks in a colander, sprinkle
with salt and allow to drain for 20 minutes. Rinse eggplant
(aubergine) and pat dry with absorbent paper.
Heat oil in a frypan over high heat. Add garlic, coriander,
cardamom and cinnamon and cook for 1 minute.
Add eggplant (aubergine) to pan and cook, stirring, for
3 minutes or until golden. Add chick peas to pan and cook
for 3 minutes or until heated through. Stir through parsley
and remove pan from heat.
To make dressing, combine yoghurt, mint, honey and
cumin.
To serve, place spinach on serving plates. Top with
eggplant (aubergine) and chick pea mixture, and drizzle
with dressing. Serves 4.

onion tart

5 onions, sliced
2 tablespoons olive oil
2 tablespoons butter
3 tablespoons sage leaves
250g (8 oz) ready-made puff pastry
150g (5 oz) soft goats' cheese
cracked black pepper

Place onions, oil, butter and sage in a saucepan over
low heat. Cook for 12 minutes or until onions are soft
and golden.
Roll out pastry on a lightly floured surface until it's 3mm
(1/8 inch) thick. Trim pastry to a 18 x 25cm (7 x 10 inch)
rectangle and place on a baking tray. Spread goats' cheese
over pastry and top with pepper.
Spoon onions over goats' cheese. Bake in a preheated
200°C (400°F) oven for 20 minutes or until pastry is puffed
and golden. Serve with a salad of mixed greens. Serves 4.

shiitake mushroom omelette

2 teaspoons sesame oil
125g (4 oz) shiitake mushrooms,* sliced
1/2 cup chopped chives
1 teaspoon miso*
1/4 cup (2 fl oz) boiling water
5 eggs, lightly beaten
cracked black pepper

Heat oil in a wok or frypan over medium heat. Add
mushrooms and chives, and stir fry for 2 minutes. Dissolve
miso in water and add to pan. Continue stir frying until
liquid has evaporated.
Pour eggs over mushrooms and swirl mixture around sides
of wok to form a thin omelette. Cook for 1 minute. Remove
omelette from pan and roll. Top with pepper and serve.
Serves 2.

baby spinach, cheese and olive pie

125g (4 oz) baby spinach leaves
125g (4 oz) small sorrel* leaves
1 tablespoon butter
6 shallots, chopped
freshly grated nutmeg
375g (12 oz) ricotta cheese
1/3 cup grated parmesan cheese
1/4 cup chopped parsley
1/4 cup chopped mint
1/2 cup chopped pitted olives
3 eggs, lightly beaten
8 sheets filo pastry
olive oil

Place spinach and sorrel in a frypan over medium heat
and stir until wilted, then drain well. Place butter in frypan
over medium heat. Add shallots and nutmeg to pan and
cook for 2 minutes.
Combine greens, ricotta, parmesan, parsley, mint, olives
and eggs in a large bowl. Brush filo with a little olive oil and
place sheets, overlapping and overhanging, around a large
pie dish. Pour in filling, fold over excess filo and bunch
pastry to make a rim around the pie. Bake in a preheated
180°C (350°F) oven for 35 minutes or until pie is set.
Serves 6.

asparagus with sweet sake and ginger

2 teaspoons oil
2 tablespoons shredded ginger
4 shallots, chopped
1/2 cup (4 fl oz) sweet sake* or mirin*
2 tablespoons light soy sauce
1 tablespoon oyster sauce
500g (1 lb) fresh asparagus
1 tablespoon black sesame seeds
pickled ginger to serve

Heat oil in a wok or frypan over medium heat. Add ginger and shallots and stir fry for 2 minutes. Add sake, soy sauce and oyster sauce to pan and cook for 2 minutes.
Add asparagus to pan and stir fry for 3–4 minutes or until asparagus is bright in colour. Stir through sesame seeds. Serve in deep bowls with pickled ginger. Serves 4.

stir-fried beans with lemon and cashews

1 tablespoon butter
1/2 cup unsalted cashew nuts, chopped
200g (6½ oz) green beans, trimmed
150g (5 oz) snake beans, halved
150g (5 oz) yellow beans, trimmed
1/3 cup (2¾ oz) lemon juice
2 tablespoons palm* or brown sugar
1 tablespoon light soy sauce
2 tablespoons mint leaves

Heat butter in a frypan or wok over medium heat. Add cashews to pan and stir fry for 2 minutes.
Add beans to pan and stir fry for 3 minutes or until beans are crisp but tender.
Add lemon juice, sugar, soy sauce and mint to pan and cook for 1 minute or until heated through. Serve with couscous. Serves 4.

sweet potato and sage tart

1 quantity or 250g (8 oz) shortcrust pastry*
filling
750g (1½ lb) sweet potatoes
1/2 cup (4 fl oz) sour cream
3 eggs
2 tablespoons chopped sage
1 tablespoon honey
2 teaspoons ground cumin
1 teaspoon grated nutmeg
cracked black pepper
sage leaves, extra

Roll out pastry on a lightly floured surface until it's 3mm (1/8 inch) thick. Place pastry in a 23cm (9 inch) tart tin and refrigerate until required.
Cook sweet potatoes in a saucepan of boiling water until soft, drain and place in a food processor. Add sour cream and process until smooth. Stir through eggs, sage, honey, cumin, nutmeg and pepper.
Spoon mixture into pastry shell and sprinkle over extra sage leaves. Bake in a preheated 200°C (400°F) oven for 35 minutes or until pastry is golden and filling is set. Allow tart to stand for 5 minutes before cutting into wedges to serve. Serve warm or cool. Serves 4 to 6.

pumpkin gnocchi

750g (1½ lb) pumpkin, peeled and chopped
2 tablespoons butter
1¼ cups plain flour
1 egg yolk
cracked black pepper
butter sauce
125g (4 oz) butter
2 tablespoons thyme leaves
parmesan cheese shavings
cracked black pepper

Place pumpkin in a saucepan of boiling water and cook until soft. Drain and press pumpkin through a sieve. Return pumpkin to saucepan and add butter. Cook, stirring, over low heat until pumpkin has thickened and dried.
Remove pan from heat and stir through flour, egg yolk and pepper. Mixture should be a soft dough. Roll tablespoons of mixture in the palm of your hand to form a flat disk. Press with a fork on one side to indent.
To make sauce, place butter and thyme in a saucepan over low heat and simmer until golden. Cook gnocchi a few at a time in a saucepan of boiling water until they rise to the surface of the water.
To serve, top gnocchi with butter sauce, parmesan and pepper. Serves 4.

pumpkin gnocchi

jerusalem artichoke hummus with rosemary bruschetta

leek and cheddar soufflé

zucchini pancakes with double brie

stir-fried pumpkin with red curry

jerusalem artichoke hummus with rosemary bruschetta

350g (11¼ oz) Jerusalem artichokes, scrubbed
2 tablespoons butter
¾ cup (6 fl oz) milk
1½ cups cooked chick peas
1 teaspoon ground cumin
2 tablespoons lemon juice
1 clove garlic, crushed
rosemary bruschetta
1 loaf wood-fired bread
olive oil
6 sprigs rosemary

Place Jerusalem artichokes in a saucepan of boiling water and cook for 5 minutes or until tender. Drain and place artichokes in a food processor with butter and milk, and process until smooth. Add chick peas, cumin, lemon juice and garlic and process until smooth.
To make rosemary bruschetta, slice bread thinly and brush with a little olive oil. Sprinkle slices with rosemary, place under a hot grill and cook until crisp. Serve with artichoke hummus. Serves 4 to 6.

zucchini pancakes with double brie

2 cups grated zucchini (courgette)
2 eggs
3 tablespoons melted butter
¾ cup flour
⅓ cup grated parmesan cheese
cracked black pepper
½ teaspoon grated nutmeg
200g (6½ oz) double-cream brie cheese
100g (3¼ oz) semi-dried tomatoes
2 tablespoons chopped chives

Squeeze zucchini (courgette) to remove any excess liquid and place in a bowl with eggs, butter, flour, parmesan, pepper and nutmeg. Mix until smooth. Heat a non-stick frypan over medium heat. Add spoonfuls of mixture and cook for 2 minutes on each side or until pancakes are golden. Keep pancakes warm and repeat cooking process with remaining mixture.
To serve, spread a little double-cream brie over pancakes, and top with semi-dried tomatoes and chives. Serves 4.

leek and cheddar soufflé

2 tablespoons olive oil
3 leeks, chopped
2 tablespoons butter
3 tablespoons plain flour
1¼ cups (10 fl oz) milk, warmed
¾ cup grated aged cheddar cheese
1 tablespoon lemon thyme leaves
cracked black pepper
3 egg yolks
4 egg whites
1½ cups (12 fl oz) cream

Heat olive oil in a frypan over medium heat. Add leeks and cook for 6 minutes or until golden. Set aside.
Place butter in a saucepan over medium heat and melt. Add flour and cook, stirring, for 1 minute. Whisk milk into flour mixture and then stir until mixture has boiled and thickened. Remove mixture from heat and stir through cheddar, thyme, pepper, leeks and egg yolks.
Beat egg whites until soft peaks form. Fold egg whites through cheese mixture and spoon into six 1-cup capacity greased soufflé ramekins.* Place ramekins in a baking dish and fill dish with enough water to come halfway up the sides of the ramekins. Bake at 180°C (350°F) for 20 minutes or until soufflés are puffed and set. Remove baking dish from oven and allow soufflés to fall and cool slightly.
To serve, invert soufflés onto deep serving dishes and coat each with cream. Return to oven and bake for a further 15 minutes or until soufflés are puffed and golden. Serve with a rocket (arugula) salad. Serves 6.

stir-fried pumpkin with red curry

1 tablespoon oil
2–3 tablespoons red curry paste*
2 onions, chopped
650g (1 lb 5 oz) pumpkin, peeled and sliced
6 curry leaves
1½ cups (12 fl oz) coconut milk
3 tablespoons coriander leaves
1 red chilli, chopped
100g (3¼ oz) Thai pea eggplants*
½ cup toasted almonds, roughly chopped
steamed basmati rice

Heat oil in a frypan or wok over medium heat. Add curry paste and onion and cook for 2 minutes. Add pumpkin and stir fry for 3 minutes. Add curry leaves, coconut milk and coriander and allow to simmer slowly for 8 minutes or until pumpkin is soft. Stir through chilli, eggplant (aubergine) and almonds, and cook for a further 2 minutes. Serve curry with bowls of steamed basmati rice. Serves 4.

salads

basics

Salads come in many different forms and can be served in many ways. A salad makes a great light starter or an accompaniment to a main meal. Salads can also be a meal in themselves when they contain a variety of substantial ingredients as well as leafy greens.

storage

Most salad greens store well if they are washed and a little water is left on the leaves. Wrap greens loosely in a damp cloth and refrigerate. Store them in the vegetable crisper or a cool part of the refrigerator, not the coldest part of the refrigerator. Salad greens have a high water content and therefore are not suitable for freezing.

selection

When selecting lettuce, the leaves should be crisp and tightly layered together, especially towards the centre or heart. When selecting soft lettuces such as butter lettuce, the leaves should be soft but crisp with a good, bright green colour. When selecting loose salad leaves such as baby English spinach and rocket (arugula), leaves should be crisp and not wilted with a good, dark green colour. Stems should be dry and not discoloured.

preparation

Remove any wilted or damaged outer leaves. Remove leaves individually and trim stems if necessary. Wash under cold running water or soak in cold water for a few minutes. To refresh wilted leaves, place them in a bowl of cold water with a few ice cubes.

variety

Salad greens are available in an extensive range, including baby or young vegetable leaves and Asian varieties. Different salad greens have different flavours that complement and combine with many foods to make a great accompaniment. Rocket (arugula) has a definite peppery taste with an intensity ranging from mild to hot. Watercress has a mild peppery taste and wilts quickly, so it needs to be soaked in cold water to refresh. Radicchio has a sharp, bitter flavour that combines well with a strong dressing.

serving

To ensure salad leaves stay crisp, pour dressing over salad just before serving as dressings that contain vinegar and lemon juice can make the leaves limp and soft.

mizuna

baby english spinach

radicchio

rocket (arugula)

endive

balsamic dressing

1/3 cup (2¾ fl oz) balsamic vinegar
1/2 cup (4 fl oz) fruity olive oil
1 tablespoon brown sugar
1/4 cup basil leaves
cracked black pepper

Place ingredients in a saucepan over low heat. Allow basil
to infuse for 5 minutes, and strain into a bottle. Store in
refrigerator for up to 2 weeks. Makes 1 cup (8 fl oz).

simple vinaigrette

1/2 cup (4 fl oz) olive oil
1/2 cup (4 fl oz) white wine vinegar
cracked black pepper
sea salt
2 tablespoons wholegrain mustard

Place ingredients in a bowl and whisk to combine. Store
in refrigerator for up to 3 weeks. Dressing will separate on
standing. Shake to recombine. Makes 1 cup (8 fl oz).

thai dressing

1 tablespoon sesame oil
1/3 cup (2¾ fl oz) light soy sauce
2 tablespoons lime juice
1 tablespoon brown or palm sugar*
2 red chillies, chopped
1 teaspoon fish sauce,* optional

Place ingredients in a bowl and mix to combine.
Refrigerate for up to 1 week. Makes ½ cup (4 fl oz).

caesar dressing

¾ cup (6 fl oz) whole-egg mayonnaise
½ cup (4 fl oz) sour cream
2 tablespoons wholegrain mustard
1/3 cup grated parmesan cheese
cracked black pepper
4 anchovies, chopped (optional)

Combine all ingredients in a bowl and mix well. Store
in refrigertor for up to 1 week. Makes 1½ cups (12 fl oz).

balsamic octopus salad with basil   warm salad of sautéed black olives

grilled chicken and fig salad

warm red lentil salad

seared oyster salad

rocket and sweet potato salad

sweet fennel and pomegranate salad

warm red lentil salad

2 teaspoons oil
2 teaspoons cumin seeds
2 cloves garlic, cruched
2 teaspoons grated ginger
1½ cups red lentils
3 cups (24 fl oz) vegetable or chicken stock
2 tablespoons chopped mint
2 tablespoons chopped coriander
150g (5 oz) baby spinach leaves
100g (3¼ oz) goats' cheese
cracked black pepper
lime wedges

Heat oil in a saucepan over medium heat. Add cumin seeds, garlic and ginger to pan and cook for 2 minutes. Add lentils to pan and cook for 1 minute. Add stock 1 cup at a time until liquid has been absorbed. This could take about 20 minutes. Remove pan from heat and stir mint and coriander through lentils.
To serve, place spinach leaves in serving bowls, and top with lentils and goats' cheese. Sprinkle salad with pepper and serve with lime. Serves 4.

rocket and sweet potato salad

450g (14¼ oz) sweet potatoes, peeled
200g (6½ oz) haloumi*
chilli oil*
200g (6½ oz) rocket (arugula) leaves
2 tablespoons Vietnamese mint* leaves
4 shallots, shredded
dressing
1 red chilli, sliced
2 tablespoons soy sauce
2 tablespoons kaffir lime* or lime juice
2 teaspoons palm* or brown sugar

Brush sweet potatoes and haloumi with chilli oil. Cook on a preheated char grill for 1–2 minutes on each side or until sweet potatoes and haloumi are brown. Arrange rocket (arugula), mint and shallots on a serving plate. Top with sweet potatoes and haloumi. To make dressing, combine chilli, soy sauce, lime juice and sugar, and mix well. Pour dressing over salad and serve. Serves 4.

seared oyster salad

2 bunches rocket (arugula), trimmed
4 shallots, shredded
100g (3¼ oz) parmesan cheese shavings
1 cucumber, sliced thinly
24 fresh oysters in half shell
2 tablespoons butter
2 tablespoons oil
1 tablespoon lemon thyme
½ cup rice flour
2 tablespoons lemon juice
cracked black pepper

Arrange rocket (arugula), shallots, parmesan and cucumber on serving plates. Remove oysters from shells and set aside.
Heat butter, oil and lemon thyme in a small frypan over medium heat.
Press both sides of oyster lightly into flour and shake away any excess flour.
Sear oysters in hot butter mixture for 5 seconds on each side. Place oysters on rocket (arugula) salad. Add lemon juice and pepper to pan and simmer for 1 minute.
Pour pan juices over salad as a dressing and serve immediately. Serves 4.

sweet fennel and pomegranate salad

4 fennel bulbs
seeds from 1 pomegranate
100g (3¼ oz) snow pea leaves or sprouts
1 yellow capsicum (pepper), sliced
150g (5 oz) goats' cheese, sliced
dressing
3 tablespoons pomegranate juice
2 tablespoons balsamic vinegar
cracked black pepper

Trim fennel and remove tough outer pieces. Cut fennel in half and thinly slice.
Place fennel, pomegranate seeds, snow pea leaves or sprouts, capsicum (pepper) and goats' cheese in a bowl. Toss salad gently to combine and place on serving plates. To make dressing, combine pomegranate juice, vinegar and pepper, and pour over salad. Serves 4.

balsamic octopus salad with basil

500g (1 lb) baby octopus, cleaned and halved
1/4 cup (2 fl oz) balsamic vinegar
1/4 cup (2 fl oz) dry white wine
2 tablespoons honey
cracked black pepper
1 eggplant (aubergine), sliced
1 yellow capsicum (pepper), sliced
olive oil
150g (5 oz) endive
1 cup basil leaves
1 tablespoon oil

Place octopus, vinegar, wine, honey and pepper in a bowl and mix to combine. Refrigerate for 30 minutes.
Brush eggplant (aubergine) and capsicum (pepper) with olive oil and cook on a preheated barbecue or char grill until soft. Set aside. Drain octopus and cook on a hot barbecue or char grill for 1–2 minutes or until tender.
To serve, place endive and half the basil leaves on serving plates. Top with eggplant (aubergine), capsicum (pepper) and octopus. Heat oil in a frypan over medium heat and fry remaining basil until crisp. Sprinkle fried basil over salad. Serves 4.

warm salad of sautéed black olives

2 cups dry salted olives*
2 tablespoons olive oil
4 baby leeks, sliced lengthwise
2 tablespoons chopped oregano
1 tablespoon lemon juice
2 tablespoons balsamic vinegar
200g (6½ oz) baked ricotta cheese
2 roasted yellow capsicums (peppers)
cracked black pepper
wood-fired bread

Place olives in a bowl, cover them with water and allow to stand for 30 minutes. Drain. Place olive oil in a frypan over high heat. Add leeks and cook until they are well browned and soft.
Add olives, oregano, lemon juice and balsamic vinegar to pan and sauté for 3 minutes.
Place sautéed olives on a plate and serve with a wedge of baked ricotta, roasted yellow capsicums (peppers), cracked black pepper and crusty wood-fired bread. Serves 4.

grilled chicken and fig salad

2 chicken breast fillets
1 eggplant (aubergine), sliced
olive oil
8 radicchio leaves
6 figs, halved
dressing
1/3 cup (2¾ fl oz) lemon juice
2 tablespoons honey
2 tablespoons marjoram leaves
cracked black pepper

Brush chicken and eggplant (aubergine) with olive oil and cook on a preheated char grill or barbecue for 2 minutes on each side or until chicken is cooked through. Set aside.
Place radicchio leaves on serving plates. Slice chicken and place on radicchio.
Top chicken with eggplant (aubergine) and figs.
To make dressing, place lemon juice, honey, marjoram and pepper in a small saucepan over low heat and cook for 2 minutes or until mixture is warm. Pour dressing over salad and serve. Serves 4.

baby spinach and prosciutto salad

12 slices prosciutto
6 Roma tomatoes, halved
olive oil
cracked black pepper
200g (6½ oz) baby spinach leaves
200g (6½ oz) fresh asparagus, blanched*
½ cup parmesan cheese shavings
dressing
2 tablespoons olive oil
2 tablespoons lemon juice
1/4 cup basil leaves, shredded
2 teaspoons brown sugar

Place prosciutto and tomatoes, cut side up, on a baking dish, and sprinkle with olive oil and pepper. Bake at 180°C (350°F) for 25 minutes or until prosciutto is crisp and tomatoes are soft.
Arrange spinach and asparagus on serving plates. Top with tomatoes, prosciutto and parmesan.
To make dressing, combine olive oil, lemon juice, basil and sugar, and pour over salad. Serves 4.

baby spinach and prosciutto salad

roast pumpkin and couscous salad

green olive and ruby grapefruit salad

asian tuna salad

rocket, blue cheese and fried pear salad

roast pumpkin and couscous salad

500g (1 lb) pumpkin, sliced
olive oil
sea salt
1 cup couscous
1¼ cups (10 fl oz) boiling water or vegetable stock
2 tablespoons butter
125g (4 oz) green beans, trimmed
⅓ cup mint leaves
dressing
½ cup (4 fl oz) yoghurt
2 teaspoons ground cumin
2 tablespoons chopped mint
1 tablespoon honey

Place pumpkin in a baking dish and toss with a little olive oil and sea salt. Bake in a preheated 200°C (400°F) oven for 30 minutes or until pumpkin is golden and soft. Set aside. Place couscous in a bowl and pour over boiling water or vegetable stock. Add butter to couscous and allow bowl to stand for 5 minutes or until water has been absorbed. Blanch* beans in boiling water, drain and cool. Place couscous, pumpkin, beans and mint in a bowl and toss to combine. To make dressing, combine yoghurt, cumin, mint and honey. To serve, place salad on plates and pour over dressing. Serves 4.

asian tuna salad

350g (11¼ oz) tuna steak
3 tablespoons soy sauce
1 teaspoon wasabi* paste
1 tablespoon sake* or dry white wine
1 bunch mizuna, trimmed
150g (5 oz) yellow pear tomatoes, halved
1 cucumber, chopped
dressing
2 tablespoons soy sauce, extra
1 tablespoon lime juice
2 teaspoons brown sugar
2 teaspoons sesame oil

Cut tuna into chunks and combine with soy sauce, wasabi and sake. Allow tuna to marinate for 10 minutes. Arrange mizuna, tomatoes and cucumber on serving plates. To make dressing, combine soy sauce, lime juice, sugar and oil.
Heat a non-stick frypan over high heat. Cook tuna pieces in frypan for 5 seconds on each side or until seared. Place tuna on salad and top with dressing. Serves 4.

green olive and ruby grapefruit salad

250g (8 oz) green olives
2 ruby grapefruit, sliced
3 tablespoons flat-leaf (Italian) parsley leaves
2 cups watercress sprigs
½ cup roasted hazelnuts
1 avocado, chopped
1 tablespoon pomegranate molasses*
2 tablespoons olive oil
cracked black pepper

Place olives between kitchen towels and hit each olive with a mallet or rolling pin to release stone. Remove stones from olive flesh and discard.
Place olives, grapefruit, parsley, watercress, hazelnuts and avocado on a serving plate.
Mix together molasses, oil and pepper, and pour over salad. Allow salad to stand for 30 minutes before serving. Serves 4.

rocket, blue cheese and fried pear salad

8 long, thin slices bread
olive oil
⅓ cup grated parmesan cheese
2 tablespoons butter
1 tablespoon brown sugar
½ teaspoon cracked black pepper
1 tablespoon coriander leaves
2 pears, peeled and sliced
200g (6½ oz) rocket (arugula) leaves
1 cucumber, sliced
1 red onion, sliced
200g (6½ oz) soft blue cheese
cracked black pepper

Brush bread with a little olive oil and sprinkle with parmesan. Place bread on a baking tray and cook in a preheated 180°C (350°F) oven for 15 minutes or until golden and crisp. Set aside to cool.
Heat butter in a frypan over medium heat. Add brown sugar, pepper and coriander to pan and cook for 1 minute. Add pears to pan and cook for 2 minutes on each side or until golden.
To serve, arrange crisp bread, rocket (arugula), cucumber, red onion and blue cheese on serving plates.
Top with pears and pour pan juices from pears over salad. Sprinkle with cracked black pepper and serve immediately, while bread is crisp. Serves 4.

meat

basics

Different cuts of meat suit different cooking methods. There are two main methods: dry heat, which includes char grilling and stir frying, and moist heat, which includes casseroles and curries. Dry-heat methods need tender cuts while moist-heat methods give much better results with tougher cuts cooked over a longer time.

pan frying

This is a hot, quick method that requires tender cuts of meat. Ensure pan is well heated over medium heat for a few minutes before cooking. To avoid oil splattering during cooking, brush meat, not pan, with oil.

CUTS TO USE

Beef: rump, fillet, scotch fillet or porterhouse, T-bone, marinated blade.
Lamb: boneless leg steaks, cutlets, loin chops, chump chops, fillet.
Pork: fillet, butterfly steaks, schnitzel, cutlets.

casseroles/currying

These are slow, moist-heat methods that require tougher cuts of meat that tenderise well when simmered in a liquid. Tender cuts are not suitable as the meat does not break down as well as the tougher cuts. When cooking with a liquid, allow mixture to simmer but do not allow it to boil.

CUTS TO USE

Beef: blade, chuck, skin on the bone (osso bucco).
Lamb: shoulder, shank.
Pork: forequarter.

selection

Meat should have a moist, red surface with no signs of drying or surface film. The fat should be a creamy white colour and should not be dry. Look for even, well-cut meat free from sinew and excess fat.

storage

Meat is best stored loosely wrapped on a plate in the coldest part of the refrigerator so the air can circulate around it. If meat is tightly wrapped it will 'sweat'. Meat should be either cooked or frozen within 2–3 days of purchase. When freezing meat, wrap it very tightly or seal it in a plastic bag to prevent air spoilage or freezer burn. Also, don't pile pieces on top of each other but be sure to pack meat as flat as possible so it freezes quickly, which will ensure its texture is not spoiled. Meat should be completely thawed before cooking. Thaw meat on a tray in the refrigerator.

stir frying

This is a very hot, quick method of cooking and requires tender cuts of meat or strips of meat that have been marinated. Drain marinade from meat before stir frying and ensure that frypan or wok is well heated before adding meat. Cut meat into similar-sized pieces to ensure even cooking.

CUTS TO USE

Beef: rump, topside, marinated round.
Lamb: fillet, backstrap or boneless loin.
Pork: fillet, strips from the leg or neck.

roasting

This is a dry-heat method and requires tender cuts to be cooked on high heat quickly or tougher cuts to be cooked more slowly for longer. Meats are often best cooked on a rack in a baking dish with water or stock in the base of the baking dish to keep the meat moist.

CUTS TO USE

Beef: corner piece topside, piece sirloin, piece scotch fillet, standing rib roast, rolled rib roast.
Lamb: leg, shoulder, rack roast, boneless loin, rump piece, boned leg.
Pork: leg, shoulder, loin, rack, fillet, rolled and boned pork loin.

barbecueing or char grilling

These are hot, quick methods of cooking and require tender cuts or meat that has been marinated. Heat the barbecue plate or char grill well and allow the flames to subside.

Drain marinade from meat before cooking. Coals should be red and glowing when the meat is placed on the barbecue or char grill to cook. Oil the food, not the barbecue or char grill, to avoid smoking and splattering.

Char grilling can also be done in a char grill pan on the cooktop.

CUTS TO USE

Beef: rump, marinated topside, sirloin, T-bone, scotch fillet or porterhouse, eye fillet, marinated round, marinated blade, marinated ribs.
Lamb: fillet, backstrap or boneless loin, cutlets, marinated leg chops, chump chops, loin chops.
Pork: fillet, cutlets, marinated leg steaks, butterfly steaks, marinated ribs.

baking dish and racks

lemon thyme

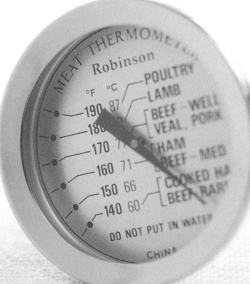

meat thermometer

forks

sage

the perfect steak

4 thick New York or sirloin steaks
oil
cracked black pepper

STEP ONE
Heat a frypan over medium heat for 5 minutes or until hot. Brush steaks with a little oil and sprinkle with cracked pepper.

STEP TWO
Place steaks in frypan and do not turn until they are sealed.

STEP THREE
Cook steaks until juices rise to the uncooked side, which usually takes about 1½ minutes. Turn steaks and cook for 1 minute more for medium rare, or for 2 minutes more for medium to well done.

STEP FOUR
Test to see if steaks are ready by pressing them with tongs. The less movement, the more cooked they are. Avoid cutting steaks to see if they are cooked, as this only releases the juices and dries them out.

variations

CHILLI STEAK
Sprinkle steaks with dried crushed chillies after brushing with oil.

MUSTARD STEAK
Spread wholegrain mustard over steaks, brush with oil and then cook.

PEPPER STEAK
Press chopped green peppercorns into steaks after brushing with oil.

PESTO STEAK
After turning steaks in pan, spread cooked sides with pesto.

the perfect steak served with chips

simmered veal shanks with wine and lemon

8 x 4cm (1½ inch) pieces veal shank
flour
2 tablespoons olive oil
2 onions, sliced
6 cloves garlic, peeled
2 cups (16 fl oz) dry white wine
2 cups (16 fl oz) chicken stock
rind ½ lemon, cut into strips
4 bay leaves
1 tablespoon chopped thyme
2 baby fennel bulbs, halved
cracked black pepper
mashed potato to serve

Toss veal in flour and shake away excess flour. Heat oil
in a frypan over high heat. Add veal to pan and brown
well. Place veal in the base of a large baking dish. Place
onions and garlic in frypan, cook until golden and add to
baking dish.
Add wine, stock, lemon rind, bay leaves and thyme to
baking dish. Cover dish and bake at 180°C (350°F) for 1½
hours. Add fennel and bake for a further 45 minutes. Serve
veal in deep plates with the fennel and pan juices, and
mashed potato drizzled with olive oil. Serves 4.

thai beef salad

450g (14¼ oz) rump steak
3 tablespoons soy sauce
2 cloves garlic, crushed
2 tablespoons lime juice
150g (5 oz) assorted lettuce leaves
⅓ cup mint leaves
⅓ cup basil leaves
¼ cup coriander leaves
1 cucumber, sliced
dressing
2 red chillies, chopped
3 tablespoons soy sauce, extra
2 tablespoons lime juice, extra
2 teaspoons palm sugar*
2 kaffir lime* leaves, shredded

Place steak, soy sauce, garlic and lime juice in a bowl and
allow to stand for 10 minutes. Cook steak on a preheated
hot char grill for 1–2 minutes on each side or until cooked
to your liking. Cover steak and set aside.
Arrange lettuce, mint, basil, coriander and cucumber on
serving plates. Slice beef thinly and place on top of salad.
To make dressing, combine chillies, soy sauce, lime juice,
palm sugar and lime leaves. Pour dressing over salad and
serve. Serves 4.

moroccan beef with steamed couscous

1 tablespoon oil
2 onions, chopped
3 cloves garlic, crushed
500g (1 lb) blade or chuck steak, diced
3 tomatoes, peeled and chopped
⅓ cup (2¾ fl oz) lemon juice
1 cinnamon stick
2 teaspoons ground coriander
4 cups (32 fl oz) beef stock
1 tablespoon oregano leaves
2 cups couscous
2 cups (16 fl oz) boiling water
1 tablespoon butter

Heat oil in a saucepan over medium heat. Add onions and
garlic and cook for 4 minutes or until golden. Add meat to
pan and cook for 5 minutes or until sealed. Add tomatoes,
lemon juice, cinnamon, coriander, stock and oregano to
pan and allow to simmer for 45 minutes.
Place couscous, water and butter in a bowl and allow to
stand for 2 minutes. Put couscous in a steamer lined with
muslin or cheesecloth and place steamer over simmering
beef. Simmer beef for a further 10 minutes.
To serve, place couscous in bowls and serve with beef.
Serves 4.

tamarind and lemon grass beef

1 tablespoon oil
2 stalks lemon grass,* chopped
6 shallots, chopped
2 green chillies, chopped
500g (1 lb) lean beef strips
3 tablespoons tamarind* concentrate
2 tablespoons lime juice
2 teaspoons fish sauce*
2 teaspoons palm* or brown sugar
1 cup shredded green pawpaw

Heat oil in a wok or frypan over high heat. Add lemon
grass, shallots and chillies to wok and stir fry for 3 minutes.
Add beef to wok and stir fry for a further 5 minutes or until
meat is well browned.
Add tamarind, lime juice, fish sauce, sugar and pawpaw to
wok and stir fry for a further 4 minutes or until heated
through. Serve with coconut rice. Serves 4.

with wine and lemon

moroccan beef with steamed couscous

thai beef salad

tamarind and lemon grass beef

rare beef and vinegared rice

coconut beef stir fry

seared beef with parmesan and rocket

steaks with red wine mushrooms

rare beef and vinegared rice

400g (12¾ oz) piece eye fillet
3 tablespoons soy sauce
½ cup (4 fl oz) plum wine or sweet cooking wine
1 tablespoon grated ginger
1 cup short-grain rice
1½ cups (12 fl oz) water
3 tablespoons seasoned rice wine vinegar
1 tablespoon oil
150g (5 oz) oyster mushrooms*
4 small squares nori,* toasted
4 shallots, sliced

Place eye fillet in a shallow dish. Combine soy sauce, plum wine and ginger, and pour over meat. Allow beef to marinate for 30 minutes. To cook rice, wash it well under running water. Place rice in a saucepan with water and cook over medium heat until water has almost been absorbed. Remove pan from heat, cover and stand for 5 minutes. Place rice in a bowl and stir through vinegar. Cover bowl and keep rice warm.
Heat oil in a frypan over medium heat. Drain beef and reserve marinade. Place beef in frypan and cook for 1 minute on each side. Remove beef from pan and cover. Place reserved marinade in frypan, add mushrooms and simmer until marinade has reduced and mushrooms are soft.
To serve, place nori on serving plates and top with rice and shallots. Thinly slice beef and place slices on rice. Top with mushrooms and reduced marinade. Serves 4.

coconut beef stir fry

1 tablespoon oil
1 stalk lemon grass,* bruised
4 pieces galangal*
2 red chillies, sliced
3 coriander roots
500g (1 lb) beef strips
8 kaffir lime* leaves, shredded
1 cup (8 fl oz) coconut cream
2 teaspoons fish sauce*
2 teaspoons brown or palm sugar*
½ cup Thai basil* leaves

Heat oil in a wok over medium heat. Add lemon grass, galangal, chillies and coriander roots and cook for 1 minute. Add beef to wok and stir fry for 4 minutes or until well browned.
Add lime leaves, coconut cream, fish sauce and sugar to wok and cook for 2 minutes. Stir through basil and serve on steamed rice. Serves 4.

seared beef with parmesan and rocket

1 tablespoon olive oil
2 red onions, thickly sliced
500g (1 lb) piece sirloin steak
cracked black pepper
150g (5 oz) rocket (arugula), trimmed
½ cup parmesan cheese shavings
3 tablespoons flat-leaf (Italian) parsley
2 tablespoons balsamic vinegar
2 tablespoons olive oil, extra

Heat olive oil in a frypan over medium heat. Add onions and cook for 5 minutes on each side or until well browned, and set aside. Slice beef into 8 steaks about 1cm (½ inch) thick. Sprinkle beef steaks with pepper. Increase heat under frypan to high. Add steaks to pan and cook for 30 seconds to 1 minute on each side or until they are sealed and seared.
To serve, toss together rocket (arugula), parmesan, parsley, balsamic vinegar and olive oil. Place 1 piece of steak on a warmed serving plate. Top steak with a little of the rocket (arugula) mixture and another steak. Add more rocket (arugula) and finish with fried onion. Serves 4.

steaks with red wine mushrooms

1 tablespoon oil
4 thick sirloin or fillet steaks
1 tablespoon butter
4 shallots, chopped
2 cloves garlic, crushed
100g (3¼ oz) shiitake mushrooms*
100g (3¼ oz) small field mushrooms
1 cup (8 fl oz) beef stock
1 cup (8 fl oz) red wine
1 tablespoon thyme leaves
cracked black pepper
mashed potato to serve

Heat oil in a frypan over medium heat. Add steaks to pan and cook for 3 minutes on each side or until cooked to your liking. While steaks are cooking, heat butter in a frypan over medium heat. Add shallots and garlic to pan and cook for 1 minute. Add mushrooms to pan and toss in hot butter for 1 minute. Add stock, wine, thyme and pepper to pan and allow to simmer until mushrooms are soft and sauce has reduced by half.
To serve, place mashed potato on warmed serving plates. Top potato with steak and pour over mushrooms and sauce. Serve immediately. Serves 4.

garlic and rosemary studded lamb

1.5kg (3 lb) leg of lamb
4 cloves garlic, sliced
4 sprigs rosemary
¼ cup (2 fl oz) honey

¼ cup Dijon mustard
½ cup (4 fl oz) dry white wine
2 tablespoons chopped mint

STEP ONE
Cut small slits in lamb, and press pieces of garlic and small sprigs of rosemary into slits.

STEP TWO
Place lamb on a rack in a baking tray and add 1 cup (8 fl oz) water to the bottom of the baking dish.

STEP THREE
Bake lamb in a preheated 200°C (400°F) oven for 40 minutes. Combine honey and mustard, and brush over lamb. Bake for a further 10 minutes or until lamb is cooked to your liking. Remove lamb from baking dish, cover and set aside.

STEP FOUR
Place baking dish over medium heat. Add wine and mint, and stir until sauce boils. To serve, slice lamb and serve with mint sauce and roasted vegetables. Serves 4 to 6.

variations

GINGER GLAZE
Use ⅓ cup of ginger marmelade instead of honey.

ORANGE GLAZE
Use ⅓ cup of orange marmelade instead of honey.

THYME LAMB
Use 6 sprigs of fresh lemon thyme instead of rosemary.

OREGANO LAMB
Use 6 sprigs of fresh oregano instead of rosemary.

garlic and rosemary studded lamb

harissa fried lamb fillets

1 tablespoon harissa* or chilli paste
2 tablespoons lemon juice
2 tablespoons chopped mint
350g (11¼ oz) lamb fillets, trimmed
2 eggplants (aubergines)
2 cloves garlic, crushed
⅓ cup (2¾ fl oz) olive oil
½ cup (4 fl oz) yoghurt
2 tablespoons tahini
3 tablespoons lemon juice, extra
4 slices Turkish bread
150g (5 oz) rocket (arugula) leaves

Place harissa, lemon juice, mint and lamb in a bowl and
allow lamb to marinate for 20 minutes. Place eggplants
(aubergines) in a baking dish and bake in a preheated
220°C (425°F) oven for 25 minutes or until skins are
charred. Peel away skins and place eggplant (aubergine)
flesh, garlic, oil, yoghurt, tahini and extra lemon juice in a
food processor or blender and process until smooth.
Cook lamb on a preheated barbecue or char grill for
1–2 minutes or until cooked to your liking.
To serve, place Turkish bread on serving plates. Top bread
with rocket (arugula) and slices of lamb. Serve with
eggplant (aubergine) purée. Serves 4.

slow-simmered lamb shanks

6–8 lamb shanks, trimmed
3 cups (24 fl oz) beef stock
1 cup (8 fl oz) red wine
6 bay leaves
4 cloves garlic, peeled
8 baby onions, peeled
2 sprigs rosemary
3 sprigs marjoram
1 tablespoon peppercorns

Place a frypan over high heat. Add lamb shanks to pan
and cook for 2 minutes on each side or until they are
well browned.
Place lamb in a baking dish with stock, wine, bay leaves,
garlic, onions, rosemary, marjoram and peppercorns. Cover
dish and bake at 160°C (315°F) for 2 hours or until lamb is
very tender.
Serve lamb shanks in deep bowls with soft polenta or
potato and garlic mash. Serves 4 to 6.

soft polenta with wine lamb

4 cups (32 fl oz) hot water
1¼ cups polenta
sea salt and pepper
65g (2¼ oz) butter
½ cup grated parmesan cheese
½ cup mascarpone
cracked black pepper
8 lamb cutlets
½ cup (4 fl oz) red wine
½ cup (4 fl oz) beef stock
2 tablespoons quince paste

To cook polenta, place water in a heavy-based saucepan
over medium heat. Allow water to come to a slow simmer.
Slowly pour polenta into water while whisking to combine.
Reduce heat to as low as possible. Stir polenta
occasionally with a wooden spoon for 40–45 minutes.
Polenta is cooked when it comes away from the sides of
the pan. Stir salt, pepper, butter, parmesan, mascarpone
and extra pepper through polenta and keep it warm.
Place a frypan over high heat, add cutlets and cook for
2 minutes on each side or until they are cooked medium.
Remove cutlets from pan and keep them warm. Add wine,
stock and quince paste to pan and simmer for 5 minutes or
until sauce has thickened.
To serve, place polenta on serving plates, top with lamb
and spoon over sauce. Serves 4.

slow-roasted double lamb cutlets

8 small parsnips, peeled and sliced
6 small carrots, peeled and sliced
olive oil
8 double lamb cutlets
½ cup grated parmesan cheese
2 tablespoons wholegrain mustard
2 tablespoons chopped basil
cracked black pepper

Place parsnips and carrots on a baking tray, sprinkle with
olive oil and bake at 200°C (400°F) for 30 minutes.
Preheat a large frypan over medium heat. Add lamb cutlets
to pan and cook for 1 minute on each side or until they are
sealed and brown. Remove cutlets from pan.
Combine parmesan, mustard, basil and pepper, and spread
over lamb cutlets. Place cutlets on a baking tray and
reduce oven temperature to 150°C (300°F). Cook lamb for
20 minutes or until it is cooked to your liking.
To serve, place parsnips and carrots on serving plates and
top with lamb cutlets. Serves 4.

harissa fried lamb fillets

soft polenta with wine lamb

slow-simmered lamb shanks

slow-roasted double lamb cutlets

braised lamb and preserved lemon

roast lamb loin with parsnip chips

braised lamb and preserved lemon

1 tablespoon oil
2 cloves garlic, crushed
1 teaspoon cumin seeds
6 spring onions, halved
500g (1 lb) diced lamb
2 tablespoons chopped preserved lemon
1/3 cup chopped mint
4 bay leaves
1 cinnamon stick
3 cups (24 fl oz) beef stock
4 baby eggplants (aubergines), sliced
yoghurt to serve

Place oil in a saucepan over medium heat. Add garlic, cumin and spring onions to pan and cook for 4 minutes. Add lamb to pan and cook for 5 minutes or until meat is sealed. Add lemon, mint, bay leaves, cinnamon and stock to pan. Cover pan and simmer for 40 minutes. Add eggplants (aubergines) to pan and simmer for a further 10 minutes.
To serve, place lamb in bowls and serve with yoghurt and a tomato salad. Serves 4.

roast lamb loin with parsnip chips

500g (1 lb) boneless lamb loin
4 cloves garlic, crushed
2 tablespoons seeded mustard
2 tablespoons chopped mint
1 tablespoon chopped coriander
1 tablespoon olive oil
500g (1 lb) parsnips, peeled
oil for deep frying
sea salt
steamed zucchini (courgettes) and bok choy for serving

Trim lamb of any fat or sinew. Combine garlic, mustard, mint, coriander and oil. Rub garlic mixture over lamb and place lamb in a baking dish. Bake at 200°C (400°F) for 10 minutes or until lamb is cooked to your liking.
While lamb is roasting, cut parsnips into long thin strips. Deep fry strips in hot oil until golden and crisp.
Drain chips on absorbent kitchen paper and sprinkle with sea salt.
To serve, place steamed zucchini (courgettes) and bok choy on serving plates. Slice lamb thickly and place on vegetables. Serve with parsnip chips. Serves 4.

roast pork with apple stuffing

1.5kg (3 lb) boned pork loin
1 lemon, halved
salt
stuffing
1 tablespoon butter
1 tablespoon oil

1 onion, chopped
3 apples, peeled and sliced
2 tablespoons sage leaves
2 cups fresh breadcrumbs
1/3 cup (2¾ fl oz) milk
cracked black pepper

STEP ONE
To make stuffing, place butter and oil in a frypan over medium heat. Add onion and cook for 3 minutes or until golden.

STEP TWO
Add apples and sage to pan, and cook, stirring occasionally, until apples are golden and soft. Remove pan from heat and stir breadcrumbs, milk and pepper through onion and apple mixture.

STEP THREE
Score pork rind at 5mm (1/4 inch) intervals. Spread stuffing down the middle of the loin of pork. Roll up pork and tie it in place with cotton string.

STEP FOUR
Rub pork rind with lemon and salt. Place pork in a baking dish and cook in a preheated 220°C (425°F) oven for 20 minutes. Reduce heat to 180°C (350°F) and cook for a further 45 minutes or until pork is cooked. Do not over cook, as pork will become dry and tough. Serves 6.

variations

PEAR STUFFING
Use 3 pears, peeled and sliced, instead of apples

BASIL STUFFING
Use 3 tablespoons basil leaves instead of sage leaves.

APRICOT STUFFING
Use 6 fresh or canned apricots instead of apples.

ROSEMARY STUFFING
Use 2 tablespoons rosemary leaves instead of sage leaves.

roast pork with apple stuffing

pork, basil and pepper stir fry

2 tablespoons oil
2 cloves garlic, chopped
1 tablespoon cracked black pepper
2 red chillies, chopped
500g (1 lb) pork strips
200g (6½ oz) asparagus, halved and trimmed
4 kaffir lime* leaves, shredded
1 cup Thai basil* leaves
2 tablespoons soy sauce
1 mango or 2 nectarines, chopped

Heat oil in a wok over high heat. Add garlic, pepper and
chillies to wok and cook for 1 minute. Add pork to wok and
stir fry for 4 minutes or until pork is well browned.
Add asparagus, lime leaves, basil and soy sauce and stir fry
for 3 minutes. Stir through mango or nectarine pieces.
To serve, place stir fry on serving plates with steamed rice
as an accompaniment. Serves 4.

pork with ginger and honey

500g (1 lb oz) pork fillet
2 cloves garlic, crushed
2 tablespoons lemon juice
1 tablespoon oil
2 fennel bulbs, sliced
2 teaspoons oil, extra
4 tablespoons shredded ginger
4 tablespoons honey
½ cup (4 fl oz) Calvados* or brandy

Trim pork of any fat or sinew. Place pork in a bowl with
garlic and lemon juice, and allow to stand for 5 minutes.
Heat oil in a frypan over medium heat. Add pork and cook
for 2 minutes on each side or until well browned. Place
fennel in a baking dish, place pork on top of fennel and
cover dish. Bake at 180°C (350°F) for 15 minutes or until
pork is cooked to your liking.
While pork is cooking, heat extra oil in a saucepan over
medium heat. Add ginger and sauté for 1 minute. Add
honey and Calvados and simmer for 4–5 minutes or until
sauce has reduced by half.
To serve, slice pork and place on serving plates with fennel.
Top with ginger and honey glaze. Serves 4.

steamed pork buns

1 quantity basic bun mix*
filling
2 teaspoons oil
400g (12¾ oz) Chinese barbecue pork,* diced
1 teaspoon grated ginger
2 shallots, chopped
2 tablespoons soy sauce
1 tablespoon oyster sauce
½ cup (4 fl oz) chicken stock
2 teaspoons sugar
1 tablespoon cornflour (cornstarch)
2 tablespoons water

To make filling, place oil in a hot wok. Add pork, ginger and
shallots and stir fry for 2 minutes. Add soy sauce, oyster
sauce, stock and sugar to wok. Blend cornflour
(cornstarch) and water until smooth and add to wok,
stirring until mixture is very thick. Allow to cool.
Divide dough into 24 pieces and flatten each piece in the
palm of your hand. Place a spoonful of filling in the centre
of each and press dough edges together to form a bun.
Put a small piece of plain paper under each bun. Leave
buns to rise for 10 minutes, and then arrange them in a
bamboo steamer* leaving room for them to expand.
Place steamer over a wok of rapidly boiling water, cover
and steam for 12 minutes without lifting the lid. Serve.
Makes 24 buns.

pork with balsamic figs

4 pork cutlets
2 tablespoons basil oil*
1 tablespoon butter
4 fresh figs, quartered
3 tablespoons balsamic vinegar
⅓ cup (2¾ fl oz) beef stock
2 tablespoons brown sugar
mashed potato to serve

Brush pork with basil oil. Heat a frypan over medium heat.
Add pork and cook for 2–3 minutes on each side or until
cooked to your liking. Remove pork from pan, cover and
keep it warm.
Add butter to pan and heat until melted. Add figs to pan
and cook for 2 minutes or until golden. Remove figs from
pan and set aside. Add balsamic vinegar, stock and sugar
to pan. Bring mixture to the boil and simmer for 4 minutes
or until thickened and reduced. Return figs to pan to heat
through.
To serve, place piles of mashed potato on serving plates.
Top potato with pork, figs and balsamic sauce. Serves 4.

pork, basil and pepper stir fry

steamed pork buns

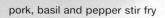

pork with ginger and honey

pork with balsamic figs

113

poultry

basics

storage

Fresh poultry should be stored loosely covered on a plate in the refrigerator for up to 2 days. Poultry is susceptible to contamination from the salmonella bacteria, which can cause food poisoning. Therefore, care must be taken when storing, preparing and cooking it. Once frozen poultry has thawed, it should be cooked within 2 days.

selection

When choosing poultry, the skin should be a light creamy colour and it should be moist. It should also be unbroken with no dark patches. The breast should be plump and the tip of the breastbone should be pliable. Free-range poultry is usually easily identified by the layer of fat over the breast and its darker or slightly yellower skin colour. The skin of corn-fed poultry has a distinctive yellow tinge. The flesh should have a fresh smell and should be free from any film. Fresh chicken is preferable to frozen. When choosing frozen chicken, be sure that its packaging has been well sealed.

preparation

Poultry does not need to be washed before cooking. Wipe the inside cavity with a damp cloth and wipe the skin if necessary. If poultry has been frozen, wipe it with absorbent paper to remove any excess moisture. When stuffing, be sure to stuff the cavity loosely so the heat can penetrate through the stuffing.

cooking tips

Be sure that poultry is cooked through. To test for readiness, pierce the flesh at the thickest part with a fork. The juices should be clear when it is cooked.

The wings and legs of larger poultry may dry out during long cooking processes, such as roasting. Cover these parts with aluminium foil to protect them from burning.

When cutting poultry to be stir fried, be sure that the pieces are similar in size, so they cook evenly.

basting

To stop the breast meat of poultry, especially chicken and turkey, from drying out while roasting, mix together butter, a little pepper and herbs of your choice. Separate skin from breast meat and rub butter mixture under the skin before roasting. This will keep the breast meat moist and tender.

freezing

When freezing poultry, wrap it well in plastic wrap or seal it in a freezer bag, and date and label it. Freeze poultry for no longer than 3 months. Frozen poultry must be thawed in the refrigerator, not at room temperature. Ensure that poultry is fully defrosted before cooking.

string

tongs

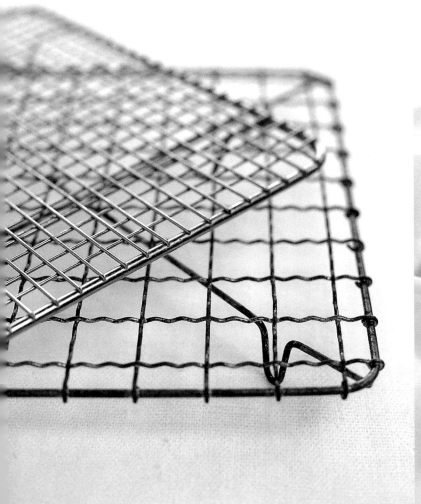

baking racks

basting brush

bay leaves

STEP ONE

Wipe and pat dry chicken. Make sure cavity is clean and any excess fat is removed. To make stuffing, place onion, breadcrumbs, parsley, basil, pepper, lemon rind, egg and milk in a bowl and mix well to combine.

roast chicken

1.8kg (3 lb 10 oz) chicken
6 bay leaves
2 cups (16 fl oz) water
oil
sea salt
stuffing
1 onion, finely chopped
2½ cups breadcrumbs
3 tablespoons chopped parsley
2 tablespoons chopped basil
cracked black pepper
2 teaspoons grated lemon rind
1 egg
½ cup (4 fl oz) milk
gravy
⅓ cup plain flour
2 cups (16 fl oz) hot water

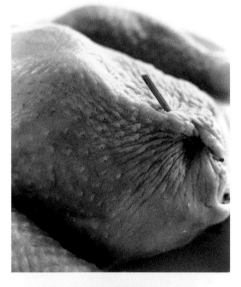

STEP TWO

Press stuffing into cavity of chicken and securely close cavity with a toothpick. Tuck wings under chicken and tie legs together with cotton string.

variations

SUN-DRIED TOMATO STUFFING
Add ⅓ cup chopped sun-dried tomatoes to stuffing.

OLIVE STUFFING
Add ⅓ cup chopped pitted olives to stuffing.

TANDOORI CHICKEN
Mix together 3 tablespoons of tandoori paste and ½ cup thick plain yoghurt. Spread mixture over chicken before roasting.

STEP THREE

Place chicken on a rack lined with bay leaves in a baking dish. Place 2 cups (16 fl oz) of water in the bottom of the baking dish. Brush chicken with a little oil and sprinkle with a little salt. Bake chicken in a preheated 200ºC (400ºF) oven for 1 hour and 15 minutes or until it is cooked through. Place chicken on a warmed plate and cover to keep warm.

PEPPER CHICKEN
Mix together 2 tablespoons of butter and 1 tablespoon of cracked black pepper. Rub mixture over chicken before baking.

STEP FOUR

To make gravy, skim the fat from the pan juices with a spoon. Sprinkle flour over pan juices and stir with a fork until smooth. Place pan over high heat and cook, stirring, for 2 minutes. Add hot water and mix until smooth. Cook, stirring, until gravy has simmered and thickened. To serve, carve chicken and serve with gravy and roast vegetables. Serves 4.

roast chicken

chicken and lime leaf stir fry

2 teaspoons sesame oil

6 shallots, chopped

1 tablespoon shredded ginger

8 kaffir lime* leaves, shredded

4 chicken breast fillets, sliced into strips

2 tablespoons soy sauce

2 tablespoons mirin* or sweet white wine

1 teaspoon red miso*

250g (8 oz) baby bok choy, chopped

4 tablespoons Thai basil*

Heat oil in a wok or frypan over high heat. Add shallots, ginger and lime leaves to wok, and stir fry for 1 minute. Add chicken strips to wok and stir fry for 3 minutes or until chicken is browned.
Add soy sauce, mirin, miso and bok choy to wok and stir fry for 3 minutes or until bok choy is tender. Stir through basil and serve immediately with steamed rice. Serves 4.

coconut chicken curry

2 teaspoons oil

1 onion, finely chopped

1 tablespoon ginger, shredded

1 stalk lemon grass,* chopped

2–3 tablespoons green curry paste*

6 kaffir lime* leaves, shredded

4 chicken breast fillets, halved

2¹/₂ cups (20 fl oz) coconut milk

¹/₃ cup basil leaves

¹/₃ cup coriander leaves

Heat oil in a saucepan over medium heat. Add onion, ginger and lemon grass and cook for 4 minutes or until onion is soft and golden. Add curry paste and lime leaves to pan and cook, stirring, for 2 minutes.
Add chicken and coconut milk to pan and allow to simmer for 20 minutes. Stir through basil and coriander. Serve with steamed jasmine rice. Serves 4.

spiced roast chicken

1.6kg (3¹/₄ lb) chicken

60g (2 oz) butter, melted

2 tablespoons soy sauce

2 tablespoons honey

4 cinnamon sticks

4 star anise

4 cardamom pods, bruised

4 cloves garlic, peeled

Halve chicken by cutting down backbone and breastbone. Place chicken halves on sheets of baking paper. Combine butter, soy sauce and honey and brush well over chicken. Top chicken with cinnamon sticks, star anise, cardamom and garlic. Fold paper over chicken and seal. Place chicken in a baking dish and bake in a preheated 200°C (400°F) oven for 35 minutes or until chicken is tender and cooked through. Serves 4.

roast beetroot with chicken

12 baby beetroot, scrubbed

olive oil

sea salt

2 cinnamon sticks

6 cardamom pods

4 chicken breast fillets, skin on

sea salt

2 tablespoons butter

1 tablespoon balsamic vinegar

2 teaspoons oregano leaves

200g (6¹/₂ oz) small beet (beetroot) tops

150g (5 oz) marinated feta

Place beetroot in a large baking dish, and sprinkle with a little olive oil and sea salt. Add cinnamon and cardamom to dish and bake at 180°C (350°F) for 40 minutes. Rub chicken skin with a little salt. Place fillets, skin side down, in a preheated frypan and brown for 3 minutes. Place chicken, skin side up, in dish with beetroot and cook for a further 15 minutes. To serve, place butter, balsamic vinegar and oregano in a small saucepan and heat until bubbling. Place chicken, beetroot and beet (beetroot) tops on serving plates and sprinkle with feta. Spoon butter mixture over beet (beetroot) tops and serve. Serves 4.

chilli chicken burritos

4 tortillas*

salad greens

2 chicken breast fillets, cooked and shredded

6 red chillies, chopped

¹/₂ cup sugar

¹/₄ cup (2 fl oz) water

2 tablespoons lime juice

1 teaspoon cumin seeds

2 tomatoes, chopped

Place tortillas on a board and top with salad greens and chicken. Place chillies, sugar, water, lime juice and cumin seeds in a saucepan and cook over medium heat, stirring, until sugar has dissolved. Cook for 4 minutes, add tomatoes and cook until mixture is thick. To serve, spoon chilli sauce over chicken, fold over tortilla and wrap it in a napkin. Serves 4.

chicken and lime leaf stir fry

spiced roast chicken

coconut chicken curry

beetroot with chicken

121

chilli chicken burritos

barbecue duck and snake bean stir fry

baked pesto-crusted chicken with rosemary potatoes   roasted green chilli and lime quail

barbecue duck and snake bean stir fry

1 Chinese barbecue duck*
2 teaspoons sesame oil
4 shallots, chopped
1 tablespoon shredded ginger
1 cinnamon stick
1 tablespoon grated orange rind
200g (6½ oz) snake beans, halved
3 tablespoons sweet white cooking wine
2 tablespoons light soy sauce

Chop duck into bite-sized pieces. Heat oil in a wok or frypan over high heat.
Add shallots, ginger and cinnamon stick to wok and stir fry for 3 minutes. Add orange rind, beans, duck, wine and soy sauce and stir fry for 5 minutes or until heated through.
Serve duck in bowls with steamed jasmine rice. Serves 4.

baked pesto-crusted chicken with rosemary potatoes

4 potatoes, thinly sliced
2 tablespoons rosemary leaves
olive oil
4 chicken breast fillets
cracked black pepper
pesto
1 cup basil leaves, firmly packed
2 cloves garlic
⅓ cup (2¾ fl oz) olive oil
⅓ cup grated parmesan cheese
¼ cup pine nuts

Layer potatoes in rounds of 4 on a baking tray, and sprinkle with rosemary and olive oil. Bake in a preheated 200°C (400°F) for 35 minutes or until potatoes are golden and soft.
To make pesto, place basil, garlic, oil, parmesan and pine nuts in a food processor or blender and process until mixture is a finely chopped paste. Place chicken in a baking dish and spread the tops of each chicken breast with pesto. Bake in a preheated 170°C (325°F) oven for 15–20 minutes or until chicken is cooked through.
To serve, place potato rounds on serving plates and top with pesto-crusted chicken. Sprinkle with cracked black pepper. Serve with a witlof (chicory) salad. Serves 4.

roasted green chilli and lime quail

4 quails, halved
2 green chillies, chopped
3 tablespoons lime juice
2 tablespoons honey
½ cup (4 fl oz) dry white wine
2 tablespoons coconut* or cider vinegar
2 coriander roots
1 stalk lemon grass,* bruised
450g (14¼ oz) sweet potato, peeled
oil for deep frying
sea salt

Place quails in a shallow dish. Combine chillies, lime juice, honey, wine, vinegar, coriander and lemon grass. Pour spice mixture over quails and marinate for 30 minutes.
Place quails in a baking dish with marinade and cover.
Bake in a preheated 180°C (350°F) oven for 30 minutes or until quails are cooked through.
While quails are cooking, slice sweet potato into long, thin strips. Deep fry strips in hot oil until crisp and drain on absorbent kitchen paper.
To serve, place sweet potato strips on a serving plate and sprinkle with sea salt. Place quails on plates and top with pan juices. Serves 4.

grilled balsamic chicken with limes

3 tablespoons balsamic vinegar
2 cloves garlic, crushed
2 tablespoons olive oil
cracked black pepper
4 chicken breast fillets
4 limes, halved
assorted salad greens
balsamic vinegar, extra

Combine vinegar, garlic, oil and pepper, and pour over chicken. Allow chicken to marinate for 5 minutes.
Remove chicken from marinade. Cook fillets on a preheated barbecue or char grill for 1–2 minutes on each side or until cooked through. While chicken is cooking, place limes on the barbecue or grill to caramelise.
To serve, arrange salad greens on serving plates. Slice chicken and place pieces on top of greens. Serve with limes and sprinkle with extra balsamic vinegar. Serves 4.

grilled balsamic chicken with limes

peppered tempura chicken with rocket mayonnaise

warm chicken salad

chicken with preserved lemons

chicken, roast tomato and basil sandwiches

peppered tempura chicken with rocket mayonnaise

4 chicken breast fillets, sliced
oil for deep frying
tempura batter
2 tablespoons cracked black pepper
1 cup plain flour
1 cup (8 fl oz) soda water
1 egg
rocket (arugula) mayonnaise
½ cup chopped rocket (arugula)
½ cup whole-egg mayonnaise
1 tablespoon lime juice

To make batter, place pepper, flour, soda water and egg in a bowl and whisk until smooth. Dip chicken strips into batter and deep fry in hot oil for 2 minutes or until chicken is golden brown. Drain on absorbent paper.
To make rocket (arugula) mayonnaise, place rocket (arugula), mayonnaise and lime juice in a food processor or blender and process until smooth.
To serve, place chicken on serving plates and serve with small bowls of rocket (arugula) mayonnaise and steamed greens. Serves 4.

chicken with preserved lemons

2 chicken breast fillets on the bone
1 tablespoon olive oil
2 onions, sliced
2 tablespoons sliced preserved lemon
2 red chillies, halved
2 cloves garlic, crushed
4 sprigs marjoram
1 cup (8 fl oz) white wine
1 cup (8 fl oz) chicken stock

Halve chicken breasts and cut into pieces. Heat oil in a frypan over high heat. Add chicken to pan and cook for 1 minute on each side or until golden. Place chicken in a baking dish.
Add onions to pan and cook for 4 minutes or until well browned. Spoon onions, lemon, chillies, garlic, marjoram, wine and stock over chicken. Cover dish and bake in a preheated 160°C (325°F) oven for 20 minutes. Remove cover and bake chicken for 5 minutes more.
To serve, place chicken in bowls and serve with steamed couscous. Serves 4.

warm chicken salad

4 chicken breast fillets on the bone
2 green tomatoes, thickly sliced
1 tablespoon olive oil
cracked black pepper
250g (8 oz) baby rocket (arugula)
3 tablespoons coriander leaves
3 tablespoons mint leaves
1 cup sliced watermelon
dressing
1 tablespoon sesame oil
2 red chillies, chopped
1 tablespoon sesame seeds
3 tablespoons mirin* or sweet white wine
1 tablespoon light soy sauce
1 tablespoon lime juice

Cut chicken into pieces. Brush chicken and tomato slices with olive oil and sprinkle with pepper. Cook chicken and tomatoes on a hot preheated barbecue or char grill until tender and cooked through.
Arrange rocket (arugula), coriander, mint and watermelon on serving plates and top with chicken and tomatoes.
To make dressing, place oil in a saucepan over medium heat. Add chillies and sesame seeds, and cook for 1 minute. Add mirin, soy sauce and lime juice, and simmer for 1 minute. Pour warm dressing over salad and serve. Serves 4.

chicken, roast tomato and basil sandwiches

2 chicken breast fillets
6 Roma tomatoes,* halved
olive oil
cracked black pepper
100g (3¼ oz) baby spinach leaves
1 cup basil leaves
3 tablespoons oil
8 slices sourdough or Turkish bread
100g (3¼ oz) aged cheddar cheese
lemon wedges

Place chicken and tomatoes on a baking dish and sprinkle with olive oil and pepper. Bake in a preheated 160°C (325°F) oven for 20 minutes or until chicken is tender and cooked through. Shred chicken.
Place spinach, chicken, tomatoes and basil on half of the bread. Place cheese on remaining slices and grill under a hot grill until cheese has melted and is golden. Place grilled-cheese slices on top of sandwiches and serve with a squeeze of lemon. Serves 4.

seafood

basics

The rules of cooking fish are simple: start with fresh fish, don't over cook it and serve it as soon as it is cooked. Easy.

fish fillets or cutlets

selection

A lot of fish are sold in fillet or cutlet form, and it is not as easy as it is for whole fish to tell whether they are fresh. Fish fillets should look fresh and moist, and the flesh should be tight in texture and attached around the bones, if there are any. The fillets should be on ice and not sitting in water, and they should have no signs of discolouration or dryness.

storage

Wrap fillets in plastic wrap or store them in an airtight container. Most fish fillets and cutlets should keep for 2–3 days in the refrigerator.

whole fish

selection

The easiest way to tell at a glance if a whole fish is fresh is by looking at its eyes. It should have full, bright, clear eyes. Fish that are a few days old often have cloudy, sunken eyes. The flesh should be firm and the scales should be tight. The fish should have a pleasant sea smell.

storage

Ask your fishmonger to gut and scale the fish, as this will extend its keeping life. Store whole fish wrapped in plastic or in an airtight container for 2–3 days in the refrigerator.

shellfish

Shellfish can be divided into two groups: crustaceans and molluscs. Crustaceans (prawns, lobsters and crabs) have an external skeleton that forms a shell. Molluscs (oysters, scallops, mussels, clams and octopuses) are invertebrates and are usually protected by a hard shell.

selection

Crustaceans should have an intact shell, no discolouration around the joints and a pleasant sea smell. Prawns should have no discolouration around the head. Whole lobsters and crabs should have a good, heavy weight for their size. They should be on ice and not sitting in water. Molluscs such as oysters, mussels and pipis should be tightly closed in their shells, although pipis open and close regularly. It is easier to buy oysters that are already shucked or opened. They should be plump with a natural creamy colour and clear liquid. They should also be shiny and free from any shell pieces. Mussels sold as live should be tightly closed in their shells. If they are open, the mussel is dead. Scallops should have a creamy white-coloured meat, free from brown marking, with the roe intact. Small octopuses are the best for cooking. Look for firm flesh with a pleasant sea smell.

storage

Keep live crustaceans in a damp hessian bag in a cool place for 2 days. Prepared crustaceans should be wrapped in foil or stored in an airtight container for up to 2 days in the refrigerator. Keep live molluscs in a damp hessian bag in a cool place for up to 2 days. Clean octopuses before storing them in the refrigerator for up to 2 days. Shucked oysters should be kept on crushed ice in the refrigerator and covered with plastic wrap for up to 2 days. All other molluscs should be stored in an airtight container in the refrigerator for up to 2 days.

prawn

blue swimmer crab

garfish

oyster

scallop

131

garfish filled with sweet potato

seared tuna burgers with fried chilli salsa

lemon-fried yabbies with dill and potato cakes

garfish filled with sweet potato

12 garfish, gutted and backbone removed
flour
olive oil
filling
250g (8 oz) orange sweet potato
2 tablespoons butter
¾ cup fresh breadcrumbs
1 tablespoon chopped preserved lemon
1 teaspoon harissa*
1 teaspoon cinnamon
English spinach for serving

To make filling, boil or steam sweet potato until soft. Mash sweet potato with butter. Combine mash, breadcrumbs, lemon, harissa and cinnamon. Spoon filling into cavities of garfish and close cavities securely with toothpicks.
Toss garfish lightly in flour and shallow fry in hot olive oil for 1–2 minutes on each side. Serve with English spinach. Serves 4.

seared tuna burgers with fried chilli salsa

4 x 120g (4 oz) tuna steaks
2 teaspoons kaffir lime* juice
1 tablespoon grated ginger
2 tablespoons soy sauce
4 poppyseed bagels, halved and toasted
salad greens
fried chilli salsa
1 tablespoon oil
4 green chillies, sliced
2 cloves garlic, sliced
4 shallots, chopped
1 green tomato, seeds removed and chopped
1 tablespoon brown sugar

Brush tuna with combined lime juice, ginger and soy sauce. To make chilli salsa, place oil in a hot frypan. Add chillies and garlic and cook until garlic is golden. Add shallots, green tomato and sugar and cook for a further 3 minutes. Remove salsa from heat and keep it warm. Cook tuna in a greased, hot frypan or on a char grill for no more than 45 seconds on each side.
To serve, place bagel bases on serving plates and top with tuna steaks. Add salad greens and top with chilli salsa and bagel tops. Serves 4.

lemon-fried yabbies with dill and potato cakes

1 tablespoon oil
1 tablespoon butter
1 lemon, sliced
2 cloves garlic, sliced
12 yabbies (or small crayfish), halved and cleaned
2 tablespoons honey
cracked black pepper
dill and potato cakes
3 potatoes, peeled and grated
2 tablespoons chopped dill

To make potato and dill cakes, combine potatoes and dill in a small bowl. Place spoonfuls of mixture on a greased barbecue plate or in a frypan and flatten with a spatula. Cook for 3 minutes on each side or until cakes are golden. Keep cooked cakes warm on the coolest part of the barbecue while cooking remaining mixture.
To cook yabbies, heat oil and butter in a frypan or on a barbecue over medium heat. Add lemon slices and garlic and cook for 4 minutes, stirring occasionally.
Add yabbies to pan or barbecue, and drizzle with honey and sprinkle with pepper. Cook for 2–3 minutes or until yabbies have changed colour and are cooked through. Serve with dill and potato cakes. Serves 4.

tea-smoked baby salmon

4 baby salmon, gutted
2 limes, sliced
12 small sorrel* leaves
olive oil
cracked black pepper
3 tablespoons jasmine tea

Place salmon in a baking dish. Fill cavities with lime slices and sorrel. Sprinkle fish with olive oil and pepper, and bake in a preheated 180°C (350°F) oven for 25 minutes or until salmon are cooked through. Drain salmon on absorbent paper to remove any cooking oil.
Place tea in the bottom of a large wok. Heat wok until tea starts to smoke. Place salmon on a rack in the wok and cover with a lid.
Allow salmon to smoke for 10 minutes. (This is best done in a well-ventilated kitchen.)
Serve salmon warm or cold with a salad of greens and whole-egg mayonnaise mixed with lime and pepper. Serves 4.

tea-smoked baby salmon

garlic-baked blue eye cod

wok-fried salted chilli crab

garlic-baked blue eye cod

6 Roma tomatoes,* halved
pepper
4 blue eye cod cutlets
4 cloves garlic, sliced
1 tablespoon lemon thyme leaves
pepper
baby English spinach leaves
lime wedges

Place tomatoes on a baking tray lined with non-stick baking paper. Place tray in a preheated 180°C (350°F) oven and bake for 25 minutes or until tomatoes are soft and lightly browned.
Place blue eye cod cutlets on a baking tray lined with non-stick baking paper and sprinkle fish with garlic, lemon thyme and pepper. Place tray in oven with tomatoes and bake for 10–15 minutes or until fish is cooked.
Serve blue eye cod on a bed of baby spinach leaves with tomatoes and lime wedges. Serves 4.

wok-fried salted chilli crab

3 green crabs
2 tablespoons oil
2 red chillies, chopped
1 tablespoon sea salt
1 tablespoon cracked black pepper
lime wedges

Remove limbs and claws from crabs. Cut body portions in half and clean well. Crack claws with the back of a knife or cleaver. Heat a wok over high heat. Add oil, chillies, salt and pepper and cook for 1 minute. Add crab pieces and stir fry for 5–7 minutes or until shells change colour and flesh is white and tender.
Serve crabs with lime wedges and eat with your fingers, so the spices on the shell flavour the crab meat. Serves 4.
Note: If the crab claws are large, lightly steam them before adding them to spices in the wok.

wok-steamed scallops with broth

24 scallops
3 tablespoons shredded ginger
3 tablespoons coriander leaves
1½ cups (12 fl oz) water
1 stalk lemon grass,* bruised
2 kaffir lime* leaves
2 tablespoons miso*
2 tablespoons oil
⅓ cup Thai basil* leaves

Remove any brown from scallops and sprinkle ginger and coriander over them. Pour water into the bottom of a wok and add lemon grass, lime leaves and scallops. Cover, place wok over medium heat and allow scallops to steam for 3–5 minutes or until cooked. Remove scallops, tipping any excess cooking juices into wok. Cover scallops and set aside. Add enough water to bottom of wok to make about 4 cups (32 fl oz) of liquid. Add miso to wok and stir to dissolve. Allow liquid to simmer for 2 minutes. Heat oil in a frypan over medium heat. Add basil, fry until crisp and drain on absorbent paper.
To serve, place scallops on serving plates, top with fried Thai basil and drizzle over a little of the cooking oil. Serve with small bowls of broth. Serves 4.

wok-steamed scallops with broth

asian infused swordfish with greens

bay and chervil fried salmon steaks

crisp, spiced snapper

asian infused swordfish with greens

4 large pieces non-stick baking paper
300g (9¹/2 oz) assorted Asian greens (for example, bok choy, choy sum, snow pea shoots)
4 swordfish steaks
4 stems coriander
8 kaffir lime* leaves
4 stalks lemon grass,* halved
4 green chillies, sliced
pepper and lime to serve

Line 4 bamboo steamers* with non-stick baking paper and allow paper to generously overhang steamers. Place mixed greens in the base of steamers. Wrap a coriander stem around each swordfish steak and place fish on greens.
Top swordfish steaks with lime leaves, lemon grass and chillies. Fold over baking paper to cover fish and put on steamer lid. Place steamer over simmering water and steam for 4–5 minutes or until swordfish are cooked. Serve with cracked black pepper and lime wedges. Serves 4.

bay and chervil fried salmon steaks

1 tablespoon olive oil
2 teaspoons sea salt
500g (1 lb) sweet potatoes, peeled and chopped
350g (11¹/4 oz) parsnips, peeled and chopped
60g (2 oz) butter
2 tablespoons oil
8 bay leaves
3 tablespoons chopped chervil
1 teaspoon cracked black pepper
2 pieces lime rind
4 x 185g (6 oz) salmon steaks
125g (4 oz) baby English spinach

Place olive oil, salt, sweet potatoes and parsnips in a baking dish and shake to combine. Place dish in a preheated 200°C (400°F) oven for 35 minutes or until sweet potatoes and parsnips are crisp and golden. Place butter and oil in a frypan over medium heat. Add bay leaves, chervil, pepper and lime rind to pan and cook for 2 minutes. Add salmon steaks to pan and cook for 1–2 minutes on each side or until steaks are cooked medium rare.
To serve, place sweet potatoes and parsnips on serving plates. Top with baby spinach and salmon. Spoon pan juices over fish before serving. Serves 4.

crisp, spiced snapper

2 teaspoons ground cumin
1 green chilli
3 stems coriander
2 cloves garlic
2 slices ginger
2 teaspoons garam masala
4 small snapper, gutted
flour
oil for deep frying

Place cumin, chilli, coriander, garlic, ginger and garam masala in a small food processor or mortar and pestle and process until smooth.
Make deep slits in the flesh of the snapper. Rub herb mixture over fish and allow to marinate in refrigerator for 1 hour.
To cook, deep fry snapper in hot oil for 1–2 minutes or until fish is crisp and cooked through. This is most easily done in a wok. Serve with thin, fried potato crisps. Serves 4.

lime prawns with green mango salad

16 large green (raw) prawns
2 tablespoons grated lime rind
3 tablespoons lime juice
2 red chillies, finely chopped
2 teaspoons cumin seeds
2 teaspoons sesame oil
green mango salad
2 green mangoes, peeled
4 shallots, chopped
2 red chillies, sliced
2 tablespoons brown sugar
2 tablespoons lime juice
¹/2 cup mint leaves
¹/4 cup coriander leaves

Peel prawn bodies, leaving heads and tails intact, and thread prawns onto bamboo skewers. Combine lime rind, lime juice, chillies, cumin seeds and sesame oil, and brush thoroughly over prawns. Allow prawns to stand for 10 minutes.
To make green mango salad, finely slice mangoes and combine them with shallots, chillies, sugar, lime juice, mint and coriander.
Place salad in small piles on serving plates.
Cook prawns on a hot char grill or barbecue for 1 minute on each side or until cooked through. Place prawns on green mango salad and serve. Serves 4.

lime prawns with green mango salad

fruit

basics

seasons

The best time to buy fruit is at the peak of its season, when it has optimum flavour, texture and colour. Its price is at its lowest, also, when it's in season.

storage

In the warmer months it's best to keep fruit in the refrigerator, with the exception of bananas. (Their skins turn black but the flesh remains fine.) The fruit and vegetable compartments are the best place for fruit in the refrigerator. Berries should be placed in a bowl lined with absorbent paper and stored in the refrigerator. Fruit that needs to be ripened should be stored at room temperature and stored in the refrigerator when it's ripe. If fruit is cut, wrap it well in plastic wrap and store it in the refrigerator. Many people believe that fruit should not be eaten straight from the refrigerator, that its flavour is better when it's close to room temperature. I tend to disagree. I think there is nothing better than a cold peach or mango on a hot summer day.

selection

Purchase fruit in season that is firm and of good colour, without blemishes or bruises. To choose melons, tap them with the heel of your hand. They should sound full. Rockmelons and honeydew melons are easily tested for ripeness by their smell at the stalk end. The ends should be firm with a little movement. Apples should be firm with undamaged skin. Pears ripen from the inside out, so choose firm, plump pears with undamaged skin. Stone fruits should be firm with undamaged skin, which should be bright, not dull and wilted. Citrus fruits should be heavy for their size and have undamaged, glossy skin. Figs should be soft and plump with a sweet smell. Figs with a slightly sour smell are overripe. Grapes should have fresh green stalks and plump fruit. Avoid grapes with split skins. Green grapes are ripe when they have a yellowish tinge and dark grapes are ripe when they have no green tinge. Nashi should have good weight for their size, which indicates they are full of juice. Mangoes should have smooth, unblemished, firm skin with a wonderful smell.

preparation

Some fruits, such as bananas and apples, brown when cut and the flesh is exposed to the air. To avoid browning, brush the cut surfaces with a little lemon juice. For nutritional reasons, peel fruit only if necessary. Wash fruit well under cold running water before preparing.

apricots

nectarine

peach

plums

raspberries   blueberries   strawberry

145

apricots in sauternes syrup

almond peach galette

lime and raspberry tart

apricots in sauternes syrup

12 apricots
1/4 cup sugar
1/3 cup (2¾ fl oz) water
1½ cups (12 fl oz) sauternes or sweet dessert wine
1 vanilla bean

Place apricots in a bowl of boiling water and allow to stand for 4 minutes. Carefully drain water and peel apricots. Place sugar and water in a saucepan over low heat and cook, stirring, until sugar has dissolved. Allow syrup to simmer, and add sauternes and vanilla bean. Simmer for 5 minutes. Add apricots and simmer for 3–5 minutes or until apricots are soft.
Serve in a deep plate with honey biscuits (see page 152). Serves 4.

almond peach galette

4 peaches
185g (6 oz) ready-made puff pastry
1/2 cup ground almonds
2 tablespoons soft butter
1/2 teaspoon vanilla extract
4 tablespoons demerara sugar

Cut peaches in half, remove stones and slice. Cut pastry into 4 rectangles.
Combine almonds, butter and vanilla extract and spread mixture down the centre of the pastry. Top pastry with peaches and sprinkle with sugar. Place galette on a baking tray and bake in a preheated 200°C (400°F) oven for 15 minutes or until pastry is puffed and golden.
Serve with thick cream or ice cream. Serves 4.

lime and raspberry tart

1 quantity or 250g (8 oz) sweet shortcrust pastry*
300g (10 oz) raspberries
icing (confectioners) sugar
filling
1/2 cup (4 fl oz) lime juice
1½ cups (12 fl oz) cream
1/2 cup (4 fl oz) coconut cream
1/2 cup caster (superfine) sugar
4 eggs, lightly beaten

Roll out pastry until it's 3mm (1/8 inch) thick. Place pastry in a deep 23cm (9 inch) round tart tin and refrigerate for 30 minutes. Line pastry shell with non-stick paper and fill with baking weights or rice. Bake shell in a preheated 180°C (350°F) oven for 5 minutes. Remove weights and paper, and bake for a further 5 minutes.
To make filling, combine lime juice, cream, coconut cream, sugar and eggs. Pour filling into pastry base and cook for 25 minutes or until just set. Refrigerate tart until it's cold and top with raspberries to serve. Serves 6 to 8.

nectarine ice cream

4 nectarines, stones removed
2 tablespoons lime juice
3 cups (24 fl oz) cream
6 egg yolks
2/3 cup sugar

Place nectarines and lime juice in a food processor and process until smooth. Push purée through a sieve. (You should have 1 cup (8 fl oz) of sieved nectarine purée.)
Place cream, egg yolks and sugar in a saucepan over low heat and stir for 10 minutes or until mixture has thickened slightly. Allow to cool.
Stir nectarine purée through cream mixture, pour into an ice-cream maker and follow manufacturer's instructions until ice cream is firm and frozen. Alternatively, pour mixture into a metal container and freeze for 1 hour. Remove from freezer and beat mixture until smooth. Return to freezer for 30 minutes. Beat mixture again and then return it to freezer until it's firm. Serves 6.

nectarine ice cream

nashi with lime and ginger

simple apple tart

honey biscuits with mixed berries

fresh plum cake

nashi with lime and ginger

1 cup sugar
4 cups (32 fl oz) water
5cm (2 inch) piece ginger, shredded
3 tablespoons lime juice
rind of 1 lime, cut into thin strips
4 nashi

Place sugar, water, ginger, lime juice and rind in a saucepan and stir over low heat until sugar has dissolved. Increase heat and allow mixture to simmer for 5 minutes.
Peel and halve nashi, and brush with extra lime juice to prevent browning. Place nashi in a bowl and pour over syrup. Refrigerate for 2 hours, stirring occasionally. Serve with lime and ginger syrup, and a scoop of toasted coconut ice cream. Serves 4.

simple apple tart

3 green apples, peeled, cored and chopped
1/4 cup (2 fl oz) water
2 teaspoons grated lemon rind
2 tablespoons sugar
250g (8 oz) ready-made puff pastry
4 green apples, extra
45g (1 1/2 oz) butter, melted
1 tablespoon sugar

Place apples, water, lemon rind and sugar in a saucepan. Cover pan and cook over medium heat until apples are very soft. Mash apples with a fork until almost smooth. Allow to cool.
Roll out pastry on a lightly floured surface into a 18 x 28cm (7 x 11 inch) rectangle, which is 3mm (1/8 inch) thick. Spread pastry with apple purée leaving a 3cm (1 1/4 inch) border. Peel, core and thinly slice extra apples. Place apples on top of apple purée. Brush apples with butter and sprinkle with sugar. Place tart on a baking tray and bake in a preheated oven at 180°C (350°F) for 30 minutes or until pastry is puffed and golden.
Serve in pieces with scoops of vanilla bean ice cream (see page 174) or thick cream. Serves 8.

honey biscuits with mixed berries

1/4 cup caster (superfine) sugar
2 tablespoons honey
1/2 cup plain flour
1 egg white
45g (1 1/2 oz) butter, melted

filling
3/4 cup (6 fl oz) thick cream
2 tablespoons pure icing (confectioners) sugar
2 teaspoons grated lime rind
500–600g (1–1 1/4 lb) mixed berries

To make biscuits, place sugar, honey, flour, egg white and butter in a bowl and stir until smooth. Drop spoonfuls of mixture onto greased baking trays and bake in a preheated 180°C (350°F) oven for 8–10 minutes or until biscuits are a dark golden colour. Cool biscuits on wire racks until they are crisp.
To make filling, mix together cream, icing (confectioners) sugar and lime.
To serve, place a honey biscuit on a serving plate, and top with a dollop of cream mixture and berries. Top with another honey biscuit and sprinkle with icing (confectioners) sugar. Serves 6 to 8.

fresh plum cake

4 blood plums, seeded and chopped
155g (5 oz) butter
3/4 cup caster (superfine) sugar
3 eggs
1 1/2 cups ground hazelnuts or almonds
1 teaspoon vanilla extract
1 1/2 cups self-raising flour
1/2 teaspoon baking powder

Place plums in a food processor, process until smooth and set aside. Place butter and sugar in a bowl, and beat until light and creamy. Add eggs and beat well.
Stir plums, hazelnuts, vanilla extract, flour and baking powder through egg mixture and pour into a greased 20cm (8 inch) round cake tin. Bake in a preheated 180°C (350°F) oven for 45–55 minutes or until cake is cooked when tested with a skewer. Stand cake in tin for 5 minutes. Serve hot with thick cream and extra slices of blood plum. Serves 8 to 10.

sugar-grilled figs

6 fresh figs, halved
2 tablespoons dessert wine
1/2 cup brown sugar
60g (2 oz) butter
toffee ice cream to serve

Place figs on a tray, flesh side up. Brush figs with dessert wine and sprinkle with brown sugar.
Place under a hot grill for 2–3 minutes or until figs are golden. Serve with toffee ice cream. Serves 4 to 6.

sugar-grilled figs

butter & baking

basics

sifting

Sift flours and lumpy sugars to incorporate air into them and to remove lumps that may not break down when mixing.

flours

Flours come in a wide variety, including white, wholemeal and self-raising. Wholemeal flour gives finished products a heavier texture and wheatier flavour. Self-raising flour is plain flour with baking powder added.

whisking

Whisking can be done with a hand wire whisk or with an electric whisk attachment on electric mixers. Whisking breaks up ingredients so they combine. It also aerates ingredients such as eggs.

folding

When folding, use a metal spoon to cut through ingredients and fold them over each other, being careful not to stir the air out of the mixture.

creaming

When creaming butter and sugar, the butter should be cold but softened slightly. Melted or partially melted butter will change the texture and rising of the end result. Cream butter and sugar until they become a pale creamy colour and the mixture looks light and aerated. It's possible to over cream the mixture, so don't over beat!

beating

Beating can be done by hand with a wooden spoon or with an electric mixer, depending on instructions in the recipe. Beating ingredients will combine and aerate them. When beating, run a plastic or rubber scraper down the sides of the bowl so ingredients are well combined. Using a food processor to beat will not aerate the ingredients; it will just make them smooth. When beating egg whites, make sure the bowl and beaters are clean and dry for maximum volume. When beating cream, make sure the cream is well chilled. If it is a hot day, chill the bowl and beaters as well.

butters

Butters can be salted and unsalted. When baking with delicate flavours, unsalted butter is better. For nutty-tasting butter for friands, melt butter over low heat, remove from heat before it is all melted and stir. For some savoury sauces, heat the butter and allow it to slowly simmer until it has turned a light golden colour. When creaming butter, remove it from the refrigerator a few hours beforehand and use at room temperature. When making pastry, butter must be cold and firm to ensure the pastry has a fine, crisp crumb.

sugars

White sugar, or granulated table sugar, is the most common type of sugar and it is used extensively. White sugar is processed to medium-sized crystals. Caster (superfine) sugar has finer, smaller crystals than white sugar. It dissolves faster than white sugar and is often used in meringues and cakes. Icing (confectioners) sugar has been ground to a powder. It can be purchased as pure icing sugar or icing sugar mixture, which has cornflour and/or calcium phosphate added to prevent it from caking while being stored. Dark brown sugar, brown sugar and light brown sugar are soft moist sugars with very small crystals. They have a distinctive flavour from the molasses coating each crystal. Brown sugars are great for puddings and baking. Demerara sugar has been treated with light brown molasses, which gives it a toffee taste. Demerara sugar is also great for baking.

creaming

whisking

cup measure

spoon measure

sifting

pound cake

375g (12 oz) butter	6 eggs
1½ cups sugar	3 cups plain flour
1 teaspoon vanilla extract	1 tablespoon baking powder

STEP ONE
Place butter and sugar in a bowl and beat until light and creamy.

STEP TWO
Add vanilla extract and eggs, one at a time, and beat well.

STEP THREE
Sift together flour and baking powder, and fold into butter and eggs.

STEP FOUR
Pour batter into a 20cm (8 inch) greased, square cake tin. Bake in a preheated 160°C (315°F) oven for 1 hour or until cake is cooked when tested with a skewer.

variations

ORANGE POUND CAKE
Add 3 tablespoons of finely grated orange rind to butter.

LEMON POUND CAKE
Add 2 tablespoons of finely grated lemon rind to butter.

COCONUT POUND CAKE
Add 1 cup of desiccated coconut when folding flour through butter and eggs.

POPPYSEED POUND CAKE
Add 3 tablespoons of poppyseeds when folding in flour.

pound cake

blueberry and lemon friands

175g (5¾ oz) unsalted butter
1 cup almond meal
1 tablespoon finely grated lemon rind
1⅔ cups icing (confectioners) sugar, sifted
5 tablespoons plain flour, sifted
5 egg whites
200g (6½ oz) blueberries, frozen or fresh

Place butter in a saucepan over low heat and cook until it is a very light golden colour.
Place almond meal, lemon rind, icing (confectioners) sugar and plain flour in a bowl and mix to combine. Add egg whites to bowl and mix. Add melted butter to bowl and mix until combined.
Pour mixture into greased ½-cup muffin or patty tins. Sprinkle friands with blueberries and bake in a preheated 200°C (400°F) oven for 15 minutes or until they are golden and springy to touch. Cool friands on wire racks and dust with extra icing sugar to serve. Makes 10 to 12.

caramel puddings

125g (4 oz) butter
1⅓ cups brown sugar
4 eggs, separated
¾ cup self-raising flour
½ cup (4 fl oz) milk
caramel sauce
½ cup brown sugar
2 tablespoons water
60g (2 oz) butter
⅓ cup (2¾ fl oz) cream

Place butter and sugar in a bowl and beat until light and creamy. Add egg yolks to bowl and beat well. Stir flour and milk through butter, sugar and egg yolks. Place egg whites in a separate bowl and beat until soft peaks form. Fold egg whites gently into mixture and spoon into six 1-cup capacity ramekins.*
Place ramekins in a baking dish and fill dish with enough water to come halfway up the sides of the ramekins. Bake in a preheated 180°C (350°F) oven for 20 minutes or until puddings are puffed up and golden.
While puddings are cooking, make caramel sauce. Place sugar, water and butter in a saucepan and stir over low heat until sugar has melted. Add cream and allow sauce to simmer for 5 minutes or until thickened.
To serve, place ramekins on serving plates and top puddings with caramel sauce. Serves 6.

chocolate cake with glaze

300g (10 oz) dark chocolate, chopped
250g (8 oz) butter
5 eggs
4 tablespoons sugar
½ cup ground almonds
1 cup self-raising flour, sifted
chocolate glaze
½ cup (4 fl oz) cream
125g (4 oz) dark chocolate, chopped

Place chocolate and butter in a saucepan over low heat and stir until smooth. Set aside. Place eggs and sugar in a bowl and beat until light and fluffy (about 6 minutes). Fold almonds, flour and chocolate mixture through eggs and sugar. Pour mixture into a greased and base-lined 23cm (9 inch) round cake tin and bake in a preheated 160°C (315°F) oven for 45 minutes or until cake is cooked when tested with a skewer. Cool cake in tin.
To make chocolate glaze, heat cream in a saucepan until almost boiling, and remove pan from heat. Stir in chocolate and continue stirring until chocolate is smooth.
Spread cake with chocolate glaze. Cut cake into wedges and serve with chilled mixed berries and thick cream. Serves 8 to 10.

patty cakes

1½ cups self-raising flour
⅔ cup caster (superfine) sugar
155g (5 oz) butter
3 eggs, lightly beaten
¼ cup (2 fl oz) milk
1 teaspoon vanilla extract
fillings
whipped cream
lemon curd

Place flour, sugar, butter, eggs, milk and vanilla extract in a bowl and beat until ingredients are well mixed. Continue to beat until mixture is light and creamy.
Spoon mixture into patty-cake cases in tins until cases are three-quarters full. Bake in a preheated 180°C (350°F) oven for 20 minutes or until cakes are golden and cooked when tested with a skewer. Allow cakes to cool on wire racks.
To serve, remove a round of cake using a teaspoon and fill the hole with whipped cream or lemon curd.
Top filling with the removed piece of cake and sprinkle with icing sugar. Serve at a grown-ups' afternoon tea party. Makes 24.

blueberry and lemon friands

chocolate cake with glaze

caramel pudding

patty cakes

vanilla sugar cookies

almond shortbread

chocolate chip cookie   chocolate brownie

vanilla sugar cookies

185g (6 oz) butter
1 cup caster (superfine) sugar
1½ teaspoons vanilla extract
2½ cups plain flour
1 egg

Place butter, sugar and vanilla extract in a food processor and process until smooth. Add flour and egg, and process until a smooth dough forms.
Knead dough lightly, wrap it in plastic wrap and refrigerate for 30 minutes. Roll out dough on sheets of non-stick baking paper until it's approximately 5mm (¼ inch) thick. Cut dough into desired shapes using cookie cutters and place shapes on baking trays.
Bake cookies in a preheated 180°C (350°F) oven for 10–12 minutes or until they are light golden. Cool cookies on racks. Makes approximately 30 cookies.

almond shortbread

250g (8 oz) butter
¾ cup icing (confectioners) sugar
1 teaspoon vanilla extract
2 cups plain flour
100g (3¼ oz) toasted blanched almonds, chopped
extra icing (confectioners) sugar for dusting

Place butter, sugar and vanilla extract in a bowl and beat until light and creamy. Add flour and almonds to bowl and mix to form a smooth dough. Refrigerate for 5 minutes or until dough is firm.
Take 2 tablespoons of dough at a time and roll into crescents. Place crescents on baking trays lined with non-stick paper and bake in a preheated 160°C (315°F) oven for 15 minutes or until shortbread is golden.
Cool shortbread on wire racks and sprinkle liberally with icing (confectioners) sugar. Makes 20.

chocolate chip cookies

125g (4 oz) butter, softened
½ teaspoon vanilla extract
1 cup brown sugar
1 egg
1 cup plain flour
1 cup self-raising flour
1 cup desiccated coconut
250g (8 oz) chopped chocolate

Place butter, vanilla extract and sugar in a bowl and beat until creamy. Beat egg into mixture and then stir through flours, coconut and chocolate. Roll 2 tablespoons of mixture at a time into balls, place balls on lined baking trays and flatten slightly. Bake in a preheated 190°C (375°F) oven for 15 minutes or until cookies are lightly browned.
Cool on trays. Serve with hot chocolate. Makes 20.

chocolate brownies

125g (4 oz) butter
125g (4 oz) dark chocolate
2 eggs
1 cup caster (superfine) sugar
1 cup plain flour
2 tablespoons self-raising flour
¾ cup chopped pecan or macadamia nuts

Place butter and chocolate in a saucepan over very low heat and stir until mixture is just smooth.
Place eggs and caster (superfine) sugar in a bowl and beat until mixture is pale and thick. Fold chocolate mixture, sifted flours and nuts through butter and eggs and pour mixture into a greased 20cm (8 inch) square cake tin. Bake in a preheated 180°C (350°F) oven for 30 minutes or until brownies are set. Allow brownies to cool and cut them into squares.
Serve with strong espresso coffee. Makes 12 squares.

steamed coconut puddings with lime

orange semolina cake

banana maple syrup muffin

steamed coconut puddings with lime

175g (5¾ oz) unsalted butter
85g (2¾ oz) caster (superfine) sugar
1 teaspoon vanilla extract
3 eggs, lightly beaten
1 cup self-raising flour, sifted
100g (3¼ oz) desiccated coconut
lime syrup
½ cup sugar
1 cup (8 fl oz) water
3 tablespoons lime juice
rind of 2 limes, shredded
3 cardamom pods, bruised

Place butter, sugar and vanilla extract in a bowl and beat until light and creamy. Add eggs to bowl and beat well. Fold in flour and coconut, and pour mixture into six ¾-cup capacity, well-greased ramekins.*
Cover mixture with small circles of greased paper. Place ramekins in a steamer and steam puddings over rapidly simmering water for 40 minutes or until they are cooked when tested with a skewer.
To make syrup, place sugar, water, lime juice and rind, and cardamom pods in a saucepan and stir over low heat until sugar has dissolved. Allow syrup to simmer for 3–5 minutes or until it has thickened slightly.
Invert puddings onto serving plates and pour over lime syrup. Serve with thick cream. Serves 6.

orange semolina cake

⅔ cup plain flour
½ teaspoon baking powder
2 cups fine semolina
4 eggs, separated
¾ cup caster (superfine) sugar
½ cup (4 fl oz) olive oil
1 tablespoon grated orange rind
½ cup (4 fl oz) orange juice
syrup
1 cup caster (superfine) sugar, extra
¾ cup (6 fl oz) orange juice, extra
1 tablespoon grated orange rind, extra

Place flour, baking powder and semolina in a bowl and mix to combine. Place egg yolks, sugar, oil and orange rind in a bowl and beat until well combined. Fold egg yolk mixture into flour mixture with orange juice.
Place egg whites in a bowl and beat until soft peaks form. Fold egg whites into flour and egg yolk mixture and pour into a greased 20cm (8 inch) square cake tin. Bake in a preheated 180°C (350°F) oven for 45 minutes or until cake is cooked when tested with a skewer.
While cake is cooking, prepare syrup. Place sugar, and orange juice and rind in a saucepan over low heat and stir until sugar has dissolved. Allow to simmer for 2 minutes. Pour half the syrup over the cake.
To serve, cut cake into wedges and spoon over remaining syrup. Serve with thick cream. Serves 6 to 8.

banana maple syrup muffins

2 cups self-raising flour
½ teaspoon ground cinnamon
½ cup sugar
300g (10 oz) sour cream
1 egg
3 tablespoons maple syrup
3 tablespoons vegetable oil
3 bananas, chopped

Place flour, cinnamon and sugar in a bowl and mix to combine. Place sour cream, egg, maple syrup, oil and bananas in a bowl and whisk to combine. Add banana mixture to dry ingredients and mix until just combined. Spoon mixture into greased ½-cup capacity muffin tins and bake in a preheated 200°C (400°F) oven for 25–30 minutes or until muffins are cooked when tested with a skewer. Serve with extra maple syrup. Makes 12.

milk & cream

basics

sour cream

Sour cream is cream with a culture added, which slightly sours and thickens the cream. Sour cream is often used in cheesecakes, cakes, sauces and soups. Sour cream makes a great topping for baked potatoes and is a quick accompaniment for many savoury dishes.

buttermilk

Originally, buttermilk was the liquid that remained after making butter from cream, hence its name. It is now made from skim (reduced-fat) milk and cultures. It has a slightly acidic taste and a thick consistency. Buttermilk not only adds flavour to cooking, its acid content also reacts with raising agents, giving some baked and flour products a lighter texture.

cream

Cream comes in a variety of forms from single, or pouring, cream to thickened cream, which has gelatine added. Gelatine helps the cream hold its shape when whipped. Cream should be well chilled before whipping. Cream also comes as thick, or double, cream, which has a higher butterfat content, making it easy to spoon and dollop. Clotted cream has been heated to just below boiling point, and then cooled. It is thick and has a rich nutty flavour and, often, a yellowish crust. Serve clotted cream with cakes, fruits and puddings.

coconut cream

Coconut cream is the extract from the first pressing of the grated flesh of mature coconuts. Subsequent pressings make coconut milk. Coconut cream is a thick greyish-white milk, which is used in sweets or curries. It will curdle if boiled. To prevent curdling, gently simmer coconut cream or add a paste of cornflour (cornstarch) and water if it is to be well heated.

milk

Cows' milk is the most readily available form of milk. It is usually sold in homogenised form, which means the cream is evenly distributed through the milk. It is also pasteurised, which means it has been heat treated to kill any bacteria that could spoil the milk. Pasteurisation also gives the milk a longer shelf life.

yoghurt

Yoghurt is made by warming milk and adding a culture of safe bacteria that thickens the milk to a smooth, spoonable consistency. Yoghurt has a fresh, tangy taste. It can be made with cows', sheep's, or goats' milk. Yoghurt makes a good substitute for sour cream.

cream

milk

yoghurt

coconut cream

sour cream

buttermilk

crème brûlée

2 cups (16 fl oz) cream
1 vanilla bean
3 tablespoons caster (superfine) sugar
5 egg yolks
1/3 cup sugar

variations

CINNAMON BRULEE
Add 2 cinnamon sticks to cream when infusing vanilla. Remove cinnamon after infusion.

LIME AND COCONUT BRULEE
Add 4 large pieces of lime rind and 1/3 cup shredded coconut to cream when infusing vanilla. Strain cream through a fine sieve after infusing.

LEMON AND BAY LEAF BRULEE
Add 4 pieces of lemon rind and 3 bay leaves to cream when infusing vanilla. Remove lemon rind and bay leaves after infusion.

STEP ONE
Place cream and vanilla bean in a saucepan over low heat. Allow cream to simmer for 3 minutes, and then stand for 20 minutes to allow vanilla to infuse into cream.

STEP TWO
Add egg yolks and sugar to cream and stir over low heat until mixture thickens enough to coat the back of a spoon. Remove vanilla bean from custard.

STEP THREE
Pour mixture into four 1/2-cup capacity ramekins.* Place ramekins in a baking dish and fill the baking dish with enough water to come halfway up the sides of the ramekins. Place dish in a preheated 180°C (350°F) oven and bake for 20 minutes or until custards are just set.

STEP FOUR
Remove ramekins from baking dish and refrigerate for 1 hour or until they are cold. Place ramekins in a tray and sprinkle tops with sugar. Put ice cubes in tray around ramekins and place tray under a preheated hot grill for 1 minute or until sugar melts and is golden. Serves 4.

crème brûlées

peaches and berries in baked cream

4 eggs
1/3 cup sugar
1 1/3 cups (10 3/4 fl oz) cream
1 teaspoon vanilla extract
3 tablespoons flour
2 peaches, sliced
1 cup mixed berries

Place eggs, sugar, cream and vanilla extract in a bowl and beat until frothy. Sift flour over egg mixture and whisk until smooth.
Pour 3/4 cup cream mixture into a greased 23cm (9 inch) pie dish. Bake in a preheated 160°C (315°F) oven for 5 minutes or until cream is just set. Remove dish from oven and sprinkle peaches and berries over baked cream. Pour remaining cream mixture over fruit and bake for 15–20 minutes or until set. Serve in wedges with ice cream. Serves 6.

vanilla bean ice cream

3 cups (24 fl oz) cream
2 vanilla beans, split
8 egg yolks
2/3 cup caster (superfine) sugar
1 teaspoon vanilla extract

Place cream and vanilla beans in a saucepan over low heat for 4 minutes. Stand pan off the heat for 30 minutes to allow vanilla to infuse into cream.
Add egg yolks and sugar to cream and stir over low heat until mixture thickens slightly. (Mixture should coat the back of a wooden spoon.) Remove vanilla beans and stir vanilla extract through cream.
Pour mixture into an ice-cream machine and freeze according to manufacturer's instructions. Alternatively, pour mixture into a metal container and freeze for 1 hour. Beat mixture to break up ice crystals and refreeze for 3 hours or until ice cream has set and is firm.
Serve in chilled bowls with cookies or biscotti. Serves 6.

strawberry ice cream sandwiches

16 caramel waffles
ice cream
2 1/2 cups (20 fl oz) cream
3 egg yolks
1/3 cup caster (superfine) sugar
3/4 cup puréed strawberries

To make ice cream, place cream, egg yolks and sugar in a saucepan and stir over low heat for 5 minutes or until mixture coats the back of a spoon. Allow mixture to cool. Add strawberries to cream mixture and place in an ice-cream machine. Follow manufacturer's instructions until ice cream is thick and frozen. Place ice cream in freezer for 30 minutes or until it's firm. Alternatively, pour mixture into a metal container and freeze for 1 hour. Beat mixture to break up ice crystals and refreeze for 3 hours or until ice cream has set and is firm.
Spread ice cream over a wafer and sandwich together with another wafer. Refreeze or serve immediately. Serves 8.

baked raspberry cheesecake

125g (4 oz) sweet plain biscuits, crushed
125g (4 oz) ground almonds
125g (4 oz) butter, melted
filling
250g (8 oz) cream cheese, softened
250g (8 oz) ricotta cheese
3 eggs
1 cup sugar
1 cup (8 fl oz) sour cream
1 tablespoon grated lemon rind
3 tablespoons lemon juice
1 tablespoon cornflour (cornstarch) blended with
1 tablespoon water
250g (8 oz) raspberries

Combine biscuits, almonds and butter and press mixture into the base of a greased 20cm (8 inch) springform cake tin. Refrigerate.
To make filling, place cream cheese, ricotta, eggs, sugar, sour cream, lemon rind and juice, and cornflour (cornstarch) mixture in a food processor, and process until smooth. (Alternatively, beat with an electric mixer until filling is smooth.) Pour mixture over base and sprinkle with raspberries. Bake in a preheated 150°C (300°F) oven for 40 minutes or until cheesecake is just set. Refrigerate until cheesecake is cold and firm.
To serve, cut cheesecake into wedges. Thick cream makes a good accompaniment. Serves 8.

peaches and berries in baked cream

vanilla bean ice cream   strawberry ice cream sandwiches

baked raspberry cheesecake

passionfruit curd tart brûlée

passionfruit curd tart brûlée

1 quantity or 250g (8 oz) sweet shortcrust pastry*
passionfruit curd filling
1 cup caster (superfine) sugar
4 eggs
250ml (8 fl oz) cream
200ml (7 fl oz) passionfruit pulp
2 tablespoons lemon juice
sugar to top

Roll out pastry to fit a 25cm (10 inch) removable-base tart tin. Prick a few holes in the pastry and place a piece of baking paper in the pastry shell. Fill shell with baking weights or rice and bake at 180°C (350°F) for 10 minutes. Remove shell from oven and take out weights and paper. Bake shell for a further 5 minutes. (This process is called blind baking and will keep the tart shell crisp when it has a wet filling.)

To make filling, place sugar, eggs, cream, passionfruit pulp and lemon juice in a bowl, and whisk to combine. Pour filling into tart shell and bake for 30 minutes or until filling is just set. Refrigerate until filling is firm. Sprinkle top of tart with sugar and place under a hot grill until sugar is golden and caramelised. Stand tart for 2 minutes before cutting it into wedges and serving with clotted cream. Serves 6 to 8.

quince with star anise on sticky rice

4 quinces, peeled, cored and halved
1/2 cup sugar
6 star anise
1 vanilla bean
sticky rice
2 cups black glutinous rice
4 cups (32 fl oz) water
1 cup (8 fl oz) coconut cream
1 pandanus leaf, optional
2 tablespoons palm* or brown sugar

Place quinces in a saucepan with enough simmering water to cover them, and add sugar, star anise and vanilla bean to pan.

Cover pan and allow contents to simmer for 2 hours or until quinces are soft and have turned pink.

Soak rice overnight in cold water. Drain and put rice in a saucepan with 4 cups of water. Cover pan and cook over low heat for 10 minutes or until water has been absorbed. Add coconut cream and pandanus leaf to rice and cook over low heat, stirring, until rice is cooked through. Stir palm sugar through rice and spoon mixture into bowls.

Top with a quince half and a little of the quince syrup.

Serves 6 to 8.

quince with star anise on sticky rice

custard tarts

lemon yoghurt cake

blueberry buttermilk pancakes

little bread and butter puddings

custard tarts

1 quantity or 250g (8 oz) sweet shortcrust pastry*
filling
2 cups (16 fl oz) milk
1 vanilla bean
6 eggs
4 tablespoons sugar
freshly grated nutmeg

Roll out pastry on a lightly floured surface until it's 3mm
(1/8 inch) thick. Place pastry in 6 small pie dishes and
refrigerate for 30 minutes. Prick base of pastry and line with
baking paper. Fill the paper with baking weights or rice.
Bake at 180°C (350°F) for 5 minutes. Remove weights and
paper and cook pastry for a further 5 minutes.
To make filling, place milk and vanilla bean in a saucepan
over low heat for 5 minutes. Allow milk to stand and cool.
Remove vanilla bean. Gently whisk eggs and sugar. Add
milk and combine. Pour filling into pastry cases, top with
grated nutmeg and bake at 140°C (275°F) for 20 minutes
or until filling is just set. Allow tarts to cool before serving.
Serves 6.

blueberry buttermilk pancakes

1 cup self-raising flour
3 tablespoons caster (superfine) sugar
1 teaspoon bicarbonate of soda (baking soda)
1 egg
45g (1½ oz) butter, melted
1½ cups (12 fl oz) buttermilk
250g (8 oz) blueberries
2 teaspoons grated lemon rind
extra blueberries to serve
honeycomb butter
125g (4 oz) butter, softened
½ cup chopped honeycomb confectionery
1 tablespoon honey

Place flour, sugar and bicarbonate of soda (baking soda) in
a bowl and mix to combine. Place egg, butter and
buttermilk in a separate bowl and whisk to combine. Add
mixture to flour and sugar, and mix until smooth.
Stir blueberries and lemon rind through buttermilk–flour
mixture. Pour spoonfuls of mixture into a greased,
preheated frypan over medium heat. Cook for 1 minute on
each side or until pancakes are golden.
To make honeycomb butter, combine butter, honeycomb
and honey.
To serve, place pancakes in a stack on a serving plate and
top stack with extra blueberries and honeycomb butter.
Serves 4 to 6.

lemon yoghurt cake

125g (4 oz) butter
1 cup caster (superfine) sugar
2 eggs, lightly beaten
1 cup (8 fl oz) thick plain yoghurt
3 tablespoons lemon juice
1 tablespoon lemon rind
2½ cups self-raising flour
½ teaspoon bicarbonate of soda (baking soda)
lemon syrup
1/3 cup sugar
½ cup (4 fl oz) water
3 tablespoons lemon juice
rind of 1 lemon, cut in thin strips

Place butter and sugar in a bowl and beat until light and
creamy. Add eggs and beat well.
Stir yoghurt, lemon juice and rind, flour and bicarbonate of
soda (baking soda) into butter and eggs, and mix to
combine. Spoon mixture into a greased 23cm (9 inch)
round cake tin and bake in a preheated 180°C (350°F)
oven for 45 minutes or until cake is cooked when tested
with a skewer.
To make syrup, place sugar, water, and lemon juice and
lemon rind in a saucepan. Cook, stirring, over low heat until
sugar has dissolved.
Allow syrup to simmer for 4 minutes, then immediately pour
syrup over cake while it is hot and still in the tin. Allow cake
to stand for 5 minutes, and serve with a dollop of yoghurt.
Serves 10.

little bread and butter puddings

2 pears, peeled, cored and sliced
12 small slices panettone or brioche, chopped
4 eggs
1 cup (8 fl oz) cream
1 cup (8 fl oz) milk
1 teaspoon vanilla extract
2 tablespoons caster (superfine) sugar
brown sugar

Grease four 1¼-cup capacity ramekins* or large
cappuccino cups with butter. Place pears and panettone in
ramekins. Combine eggs, cream, milk, vanilla and sugar.
Pour mixture over panettone and sprinkle tops with brown
sugar. Allow puddings to stand for 5 minutes. Place
ramekins in a baking dish half filled with water. Place dish in
a preheated 180°C (350°F) oven for 25–30 minutes or until
puddings are firm.
To serve, place ramekins on a plate or invert puddings onto
a plate and serve with small ramekins of toffee ice cream.
Serves 4.

glossary

angel hair pasta

A very thin, tubular pasta – hence its name. Substitutes include spaghetti, linguini, thin fettuccine.

bamboo steamer

An Asian bamboo container with a lid and a slatted base. Placed on top of a saucepan of boiling water, the bamboo steamer holds the foods to be steamed. A metal steamer can also be used. Available from Asian food stores and most kitchen shops.

banana leaves

Leaves of the banana plant, used to wrap food to be cooked. Available from Asian food stores.

basic bun mix

2 tablespoons sugar
1½ cups (12 fl oz) warm water
1 tablespoon dry yeast
5 cups plain flour
2 tablespoons melted butter or lard

Place sugar and water in a bowl and stir to dissolve. Add yeast and leave bowl in a warm place for 5 minutes or until mixture is foamy. Add flour and melted butter or lard to bowl and mix until combined. Place dough on a lightly floured surface and knead for 4 minutes or until smooth. Roll dough into a sausage shape and cover with a cloth. Use within 2–3 hours. Makes 1 quantity.

basil oil

Oil that has been infused with basil leaves. Available from good delicatessens.

blanching

A cooking method in which foods are plunged into boiling water for a few seconds, removed from the water and refreshed under cold water, which stops the cooking process. Used to heighten colour and flavour, to firm flesh and to loosen skins.

bocconcini

Fresh Italian mozzarella balls sold in a water or brine solution. Available from delicatessens and supermarkets.

bonito flakes

Shaved flakes of a dried bonito fish. A basic flavouring in Japanese cuisine. Available from Asian food stores.

calvados

Dry, apple-flavoured brandy, which is named after a town in the Normandy region of France. Substitute apple cider, brandy or sweet cooking wine.

char grilling

A method of cooking that uses a ridged or slotted hot grill either over a barbecue, or on an electric char grill, in a char grill pan or a on flat char grill plate that sits on a cooktop. This gives foods a distinct, lined pattern and a smoky, grilled flavour.

chilli oil

Oil infused with the heat and flavour of chillies. It often has a red tinge. Different brands have different strengths. Available from Asian food stores and delicatessens.

chinese barbecue duck

Spiced and glazed duck. If necessary, substitute a home-roasted duck. Available from Chinese barbecue shops.

chinese barbecue pork

Spiced and glazed pork fillets. If necessary, substitute home-roasted pork fillets. Available from Chinese barbecue shops.

chorizo sausage

A spicy Spanish sausage containing a mixture of pork, pepper and chillies. Available from some butchers and delicatessens.

coconut vinegar

A cloudy vinegar made from fermented coconut juice. It is usually only 4–6 per cent acidity, which is much lower than other commercially available vinegars. Available from Asian food stores.

crème fraîche

A mixture of sour cream and fresh cream. Substitute sour cream.

dry salted olives

Wrinkled black olives. Available from good delicatessens or grocers.

enoki mushrooms

Also known as enokitake mushrooms. Thin, long-stemmed mushrooms with a mild flavour. Available from good fruit and vegetable shops.

fish sauce

Clear, amber-tinted liquid that is drained from salted, fermented fish. A very important flavouring in Thai cuisine. Available from supermarkets and Asian food stores.

galangal

A spice that looks similar to ginger and has a pink tinge. Can be purchased fresh, or sliced and bottled in brine.

green curry paste

A hot and spicy paste of ground green chillies, herbs and spices. Available in bottles from supermarkets or Asian food stores.

haloumi

Firm white cheese made from sheep's milk. It has a stringy texture and is usually sold in brine. Available from delicatessens and some supermarkets.

harissa

A hot paste of red chillies, garlic and olive oil. Available in tubes or jars from delicatessens.

hoi sin sauce

A thick, sweet-tasting Chinese sauce made from fermented soy beans, sugar, salt and red rice. Use as a dipping sauce or glaze. Available from Asian food stores and supermarkets.

japanese pumpkin

A very sweet and soft variety of pumpkin.

kaffir lime

A variety of lime with a knobbly outer skin. The fragrant leaves are crushed or shredded and used in cooking, and the limes are used for their juice, mainly in Thai cuisine. Available as packets of leaves or as limes from Asian grocers.

lemon grass

A tall, lemon-scented grass used in Asian, mainly Thai, cooking. Peel away outer leaves and use the tender root end of the grass. Chop finely or use in pieces to infuse flavour and remove from dish before serving. Available from Asian food stores and good fruit and vegetable shops.

linguini pasta

Long, thin pasta with square cut edges. Similar to flat spaghetti. Substitute spaghetti or fettuccine.

mirin

Heavily sweetened rice wine used as cooking wine. Substuite sweet white wine.

miso

A thick paste made from fermented and processed soy beans. Red miso is a combination of barley and soy beans and yellow miso is a combination of rice and soy beans.

nori sheets

Dried seaweed pressed into square sheets. Use for nori rolls, soups and Japanese cuisine. Keep dry and store in an airtight container. Available in packets from Asian food stores.

oyster mushrooms

Thin-ridged, delicately flavoured, cultivated mushrooms with a slight taste of oysters. Available from good fruit and vegetable shops.

palm sugar

Sap of a palm concentrated into a heavy, moist sugar. Sold in block form and should be grated or shaved before using. Used mainly in Thai cooking. Substitute brown sugar.

pasta

3 cups flour
4 large eggs
2 teaspoons salt

Place flour on a bench top in a mound. Make a hole in the mound and break eggs and put salt into the hole. Break up eggs with a fork and gradually add flour to the eggs until a rough dough forms. (You can do this step in a food processor.) Place dough on a lightly floured surface (you may need to add a little water or flour to make the dough manageable) and knead until it is smooth. Cut pasta into 4 pieces and roll through a pasta machine or using a rolling pin until it is the desired thickness. Cut pasta into shapes or cover with a damp cloth if you are using it a few hours later. Cook pasta in plenty of rapidly boiling water until it is al dente. Make sure the water stays boiling while the pasta cooks. To dry, hang pasta over a suspended wooden spoon or a clean broom handle for 1–2 hours (depending on the weather), until it's dry and hard. Store pasta in airtight containers.
Makes 1 quantity.

pizza dough

1 teaspoon active dry yeast
pinch sugar
2/3 cup (5½ fl oz) warm water
2 cups plain flour
½ teaspoon salt
¼ cup (2 fl oz) olive oil

Place yeast, sugar and water in a bowl and allow to stand until mixture has bubbles. Add flour, salt and oil and mix to form a smooth dough. Knead dough for 5 minutes or until it is smooth and elastic. Place dough in a clean, oiled bowl, cover and allow to stand in a warm place for 20 minutes or until it has doubled in size. Makes 1 quantity.

pomegranate molasses

Richly flavoured molasses made from pomegranates, sugar and lemon juice. A traditional product from the eastern Mediterranean. Available from Middle Eastern delicatessens and food stores.

porcini mushrooms

Mushrooms with a meaty texture and a woody, earthy taste. Available fresh in Europe and the United Kingdom, and sold dried in small packets in Australia and the United States of America. Dried porcini should be soaked in hot water before using. Substitute any mushrooms.

red curry paste

A hot and spicy paste of ground red chillies, herbs and spices. Available in bottles from supermarkets or Asian food stores.

ramekins

Small, ovenproof dishes used for soufflés and other individually served foods.

roma tomatoes

Also known as egg tomatoes. Oval-shaped tomatoes, which are great for cooking and eating.

saffron

The dried yellow-orange stigma from the small purple crocus flower (Crocus sativus), which is hand cultivated and consequently expensive. Used as a flavouring and colouring. A little goes a long way. Available in both powdered form (which loses its flavour more quickly) and as threads from good supermarkets and delicatessens.

sake

Japanese fermented rice wine. Used in cooking to tenderise and add flavour. Store in a cool dark place and use soon after opening. Substitute dry white wine.

sashimi tuna

Finest quality tuna cut in an Asian or Japanese style. It is very tender and is used raw in Japanese cuisine. Available from good fish markets.

shiitake mushrooms

Originally from Japan and Korea, these mushrooms have a distinctive, full-bodied flavour. They have brownish tops with a creamy underside. Available from good fruit and vegetable stores.

shortcrust pastry

2 cups plain flour
155g (5 oz) butter, chopped
iced water

Place flour and butter in a food processor and process until mixture has formed fine crumbs.
Add enough iced water to form a soft dough. Remove dough from food processor and knead lightly, wrap in plastic wrap and refrigerate for 30 minutes before rolling to prevent shrinkage when baked. Makes 1 quantity.

sorrel

A hardy perennial herb with a large green leaf belonging to the buckwheat family. Sorrel has a slightly acidic and sour taste due to the presence of oxalic acid. Choose bright green, crisp leaves. Readily available during spring from good fruit and vegetable stores.

sweet shortcrust pastry

2 cups plain flour
3 tablespoons caster sugar
155g (5 oz) butter, chopped
iced water

Place flour, sugar and butter in a food processor and process until mixture has formed fine crumbs.
Add enough iced water to form a soft dough.
Remove dough from food processor and knead lightly, wrap in plastic wrap and refrigerate for 30 minutes before rolling to prevent shrinkage when baked.
Makes 1 quantity.

tamarind paste/concentrate

A product from the ripe bean pods of the tamarind tree. It can be purchased as pulp or in the more convenient form of tamarind concentrate ready to use. Used extensively in Asia. Available from Asian food stores.

thai basil

Includes many varieties such as holy, purple and sweet. Any of these can be used in Thai or Asian cuisines.

thai pea eggplant

Grown as clusters of small, light green peas. It is bitter in taste and is a traditional ingredient in Thai green curry. Available from Asian food stores.

tortillas

Cornbread baked in flat discs used to wrap foods or eaten as bread. Wheat flour tortillas are another popular variety. Traditionally from Mexico and South American countries. Available from supermarkets.

vanilla bean

Cured pods from the vanilla orchid. Used whole, often split, to infuse flavour into custard or cream-based recipes. Also available is pure vanilla extract, which is a thick, dark, sticky liquid, and makes a good substitute for vanilla beans.

vietnamese mint

Not a member of the mint family although it is called mint. It has long, green, narrow leaves with purple markings. It is bitter and pungent in flavour. Available from Asian food stores.

wasabi

A spice that comes from a knobbly green root of the Japanese plant *wasabia japonica*. A traditional condiment served with Japanese sushi and sashimi. It has the same warming or stinging nasal sensation as horseradish. Available in paste or powdered form from Asian grocers.

conversion chart

1 cup = 250 ml (8 fl oz)
1 Australian tablespoon = 20 ml
(4 teaspoons)
1 UK tablespoon = 15 ml
(3 teaspoons)
1 teaspoon = 5ml

CUP CONVERSIONS
1 cup almonds, whole = 155g (5 oz)
1 cup breadcrumbs, dried = 125g (4 oz)
1 cup cheese, grated = 125g (4 oz)
1 cup chick peas = 220g (7 oz)
1 cup coconut, desiccated = 90g (3 oz)
1 cup couscous = 200g (6½ oz)
1 cup flour, white = 125g (4 oz)
1 cup hazlenuts = 170g (5½ oz)
1 cup lentils = 200g (6½ oz)
1 cup mushrooms = 125g (4 oz)
1 cup olives, stoned = 155g (5 oz)
1 cup parsley, chopped = 45g (1½ oz)
1 cup rice, raw = 220g (7 oz)
1 cup sugar, caster = 220g (7 oz)
1 cup sugar, white = 250g (8 oz)
1 cup semolina = 170g (5½ oz)
1 cup watermelon, cubed = 220g (7 oz)

index